Free Indeed!

Free Indeed!

Rod and Staff Publishers, Inc.
P.O. Box 3, Hwy. 172
Crockett, Kentucky 41413
606-522-4348

Background cover photo is by Ross Hamilton Photography, Inc., and eagle is from PhotoDisc by Getty Images, Inc.

Printed in U.S.A.

Hardcover edition ISBN 978-07399-2409-9
Catalog no. 2522

Paper edition ISBN 978-07399-2455-6
Catalog no. 2521

3 4 5 6 7 — 21 20 19 18 17 16 15 14 13 12

Table of Contents

Foreword

You have paid less for this book than what many others pay for just one hour of professional counseling. You have also paid less than what others pay for just one month's supply of special mood-altering medications.

But with the help of the Lord, you might be able to receive much more than any of the others mentioned above. Without educational degrees or titles, the author introduces basic principles from the Word of God which can give life and health. Everyone will find a part of himself lurking somewhere in these pages. You will have the opportunity to pull aside the camouflage and take a good hard look at yourself and your hidden (or perhaps known) sore spots.

Life is not always fair or equal. Offenses will come. And as part of humanity, we may be responsible for causing offenses at times. It is nearly impossible to go through life without receiving some bumps and bruises. By their presence, these things bring hurt and harm. But hurt and harm can also come by the absence of good things. For example, a child who does not know parental love will experience this second type of harm. Hurts exist in both ways, and these hurts cry for healing.

Salvation, or deliverance, is not presented in these pages as something that takes place when life is over and we reach the perfect eternal state. Through God's grace, it can be a reality here and now! Redemption that begins today will extend to and expand in eternity. There, the spirits of just men will be made perfect! But it can and must begin today.

So find a quiet spot. Open your heart to truth. With a prayer for divine direction, read discerningly and carefully. God is a rewarder of those who diligently seek Him. You can find Him in these pages.

—Harry M. Erb

Introduction

This book is an effort to encourage us in the emotional hurdles we face in life. It points out some of the snares that can bring us into emotional bondage and rob us of freedom in the soul. Satan tries to use these snares to rob us not only of our freedom but also of our own soul's salvation.

This book is an effort to understand and experience what Jesus meant when He said, "If the Son therefore shall make you free, ye shall be free indeed" (John 8:36).

All that is said is based on the conviction that God has answers for us in every area of life and that these answers normally lie in a serious, sensitive, spiritual walk with the Lord.

Therefore, this book emphasizes practical suggestions that lead us deeper into His ways. The Holy Spirit, the Word, the conscience, and the brotherhood of believers are all a part of God's provision for us in this journey. "Howbeit when he, the Spirit of truth, is come, he will guide you into all truth" (John 16:13).

This book does not pretend to address all the hurdles that can arise. Neither does it pretend to offer all the answers to every possible problem one might face. But it does give the reader things to draw from and suggestions that point to the One who not only has the answer but *is* the answer!

Dear reader, if you find yourself bogged down or bound in any of the difficulties discussed, take courage. Look to the Lord. Trust His faithfulness. Yield yourself to Him, and follow Him obediently. He has promised to guide and sustain you.

"I am the door: by me if any man enter in, he shall be saved, and shall go in and out, and find pasture. The thief cometh not, but for to steal, and to kill, and to destroy: I am come that they might have life, and that they might have it more abundantly. I am the good shepherd: the good shepherd giveth his life for the sheep" (John 10:9–11).

God bless and keep you on your heavenward way.

—D.G.B.

Chapter One

An Overview of the Emotions

"If the Son therefore shall make you free, ye shall be free indeed" (John 8:36).

Before beginning a large project, a good first step is to get an overview from a distance. This is especially true about something as intangible as the emotions. Because we all are different, we each need to gain an insight into our own emotions and let the Lord show us His way to emotional freedom. May you find this book helpful and inspiring.

God gave us emotions so that we can feel love and hatred, joy and sorrow, gladness and sadness, pleasure and pain, guilt and forgiveness, and much more. These feelings are a major part of our relationship with our surroundings. God wants our emotions to be an asset in living for Him.

Emotions are a gift from God. They link us to what is happening around us and inside us. They are our response of anger or joy, or simply make us feel bad or good, depending on how the situation seems to us. Thus, our emotions are vulnerable and even changeable.

Emotions are a powerful force that God wants to work for our good—like water between the riverbanks or like fire in the stove. When the river stays within its banks and the fire heats the house, everything is fine. But when the water overflows its banks and the fire gets out of the stove, and they go where we don't want them to go, there is devastation.

This means that our emotions can be our friend or foe. As friend, they are mastered by the will. But as foe, they can somehow get into the driver's seat and overpower our will and better judgment. And when let go, they can even become an enemy to our souls. They can loom bigger than fact and severely threaten our faith in God and His Word.

These dark emotions haunt our humanity when they take control of us. They take advantage of our weaknesses and frustrate the good we would like to do. They spoil our joy and motivation and inspiration for living. They take control of our thoughts and attitudes and hold us captive. But our emotions do not need to control us. God can help us find freedom.

In spite of how we might feel at times, emotions are intended for good. Many emotions are satisfying and give us a positive, peaceful outlook on life. They encourage us to have faith in God and a love for Him that inspires faithful living. There is great freedom and purpose in such a life. Emotions that bear such fruit are the kind we desire.

How shall a believer find his way among these good and difficult emotions? Does God have the answers for us? Did Jesus mean that He can set us free from the power of emotions that try to destroy us? Indeed He did! It is that part of His promise which is the theme of this book: "If the Son therefore shall make you free, ye shall be free indeed" (John 8:36).

To begin, let's make some comparisons to see how emotions work.

Emotions Are Like Sunglasses

Some of my acquaintances drive logging trucks. They work under all kinds of conditions. For driving in dark, snowy nights, they prefer deep yellow sunglasses. Somehow this makes the snow less blinding, and they are better able to pick out the road markers that help them keep their trucks on the road.

For driving in bright sunshine, however, they generally prefer the traditional dark shades in blue, green, or gray. These sunglasses cut out the overly bright rays, helping the drivers to focus on the things that really matter.

Like logging-truck drivers, we too have varied experiences in life. Some days are dark and gloomy, some are normal, and some are bright. A workload that stresses us one day doesn't bother us the next. Sometimes our employer seems hard to please, or our employees don't seem to care. At other times, we scarcely notice it. Sometimes we can take a disappointment easily, while at other times it grinds on us. One day we find it easy to accept the mistakes of others, while on another day, their mistakes stick like burrs.

The same can happen in the home. Spilled water at the dinner table may seem catastrophic. A slammed door sounds like thunder. Being late for an appointment becomes a crisis. Children's behavior can seem so disorderly that we despair of controlling them. There seems to be no end to all the bad things that happen. But on other days, we can take all of these in stride, with a smile.

Are all these matters the way they seem at the moment? Likely not! Many times it depends on which emotions are active—what kind of sunglasses we have on. If we are patient, persevering, and peaceful in our hearts, things look totally different than when we feel stressed, sensitive, and sarcastic.

Of course, sunglasses do not change the way things really are. They only make things more manageable and pleasant. That's how our emotions are. Healthy emotions can keep us from going down with the circumstances. We don't cry just because the children around us are crying. Stable emotions help us to pick out what is really important—the road markers that keep us on the road and get us through the day.

Trouble really begins when people wear their yellow sunglasses in the sunshine and put on their dark ones at night. Unheard of? Not at all. Have you ever—when the day turned gloomy or the tire went flat—made things worse than they were? Remember your stony face, your dry comments, and your insistence on being down, even when someone tried to cheer you up? How we cling to our dark spectacles!

On the other hand, emotions can swing out too far the other way. Instead of things seeming impossible, everything seems possible. Instead of everything being dark, everything is light and easy. At those times, stable emotions help us to be realistic. They keep us from laughing too much or getting carried away with joking and doing things we are ashamed of later. We can end up getting the things that are funny mixed up with those that aren't.

God wants us to learn to handle the down times of life in a way that we do not make it harder for ourselves. He wants to help us through the valleys of life.

God is calling us to emotional adulthood, to emotional freedom. He wants us to recognize emotions for what they are and to respond to the right ones at the right time rather than letting our emotions rule us.

Emotions Are Like Mirrors

By now you have probably concluded that our emotions are not necessarily the real us. And rightly so. Basically, they are expressed feelings that are affected by our inner perceptions and outer circumstances. That means they may rise and fall in unbalanced response to a situation. That's why we liken them to mirrors.

Have you ever seen sets of trick mirrors? The mirrors are curved, showing the person in the mirror as partly enormous and partly stick thin, with distorted face and impossible legs. It looks funny because it is not real.

Sometimes emotions get out of proportion like those mirrors, but the viewer is not laughing. He is taking the image seriously. He sees only the dark side of things. For example, his emotions take a minor physical imperfection, such as a pimple or a birthmark, and magnify it until it is all he can see—and he thinks it is all others see! Many times, however, his emotions do not focus on a physical defect, but on a mental anxiety, like a memory of mistreatment, a fear of failure, or a sense of worthlessness. At the same time, the positive things in his life are so small he doesn't notice them. Because of his morbid feelings about himself, nothing is quite right.

Or the emotions can take a person out the other side and give him an overblown image of his greatness and goodness. He may have a swollen impression about his intellect, his strength, his appearance, or his personality. The old-fashioned word for that is *pride*.

Now, let's have our emotions be a different mirror—this time a straight mirror that shows it just like it is. Nothing is more frankly honest than a good mirror. Our emotions—the good ones and the bad ones—may be telling how it is on the inside. Maybe we could call them a mirror of the soul.

While we may not always like what the mirror shows, we can't change it by polishing or smashing the mirror! We must deal with the person in the mirror! That is why we emphasize the importance of seeing life as it really is and following the facts rather than our feelings.

Emotions are supposed to be like straight mirrors. We need to measure what we see in the mirror with what the Bible says because, in themselves, emotions are not dependable. One person said, "I can feel good about myself in the morning, and depressed by evening. I doubt that my soul has changed in that time, so my emotions were wrong either in the morning or in the evening. Quite likely, they weren't really accurate either time, since my soul's condition is probably in between."

Even if we have positive feelings about ourselves (the Bible says, "No man ever yet hated his own flesh"), we should try to see ourselves and our circumstances as they are. Instead of the facts being distorted by our feelings, our feelings should reflect the facts. Rather than trying to change the emotional mirror, we must work on the things that are producing the emotion more than on the emotion itself. That is the only way to truly have the freedom God wants us to have.

Emotions Reveal Attitudes

Sometimes emotions give away things we thought we had hidden. The emotions can be as frank as a little child who says to the company, "Dad says we may as well have you over for a meal and get it over with" or says, "I know you don't like to talk to Hank on the phone 'cause you always make your eyes go up in the air when you find out it's him!" Our emotions tell on us because they slip into our tone of voice or our choice of words, and they reveal just how we feel.

"I believe you have an attitude problem toward those people," a friend once told me. Me? An attitude problem? His statement startled me! But I thought it over. And I began to fear that he was right. I felt more critical about those people than I realized. But how did my friend know? He discerned it by the way I expressed myself. So it goes. The way we feel shows in our tone of voice, in the slant of our statements, and even in our body language. Our emotions can reveal what we thought was well camouflaged. Once we are ready to correct what our emotions reveal about us, the effects will be good.

Our emotions are somewhat like spiritual fingerprints, an evident part of our identity. After all, it is the part of us that people see and feel. When you think of what someone is like, do you think about his physical appearance or do you think about his emotional disposition and personality? Quite likely, you think of his disposition first. This means that our emotions say a good bit about us.

I once met a man who had the habit of carrying a book with him and describing in it the people he met. He let me read it. His descriptions were not about physique or age. Rather, he described emotional characteristics that created vivid mental images—the kind you remember people by.

Naturally, our emotions express good attitudes too! When the heart and mind focus on good things, the emotions radiate generous, grateful, optimistic attitudes. When the heart is throbbing about the good things in life, the feelings reflect this. We could say that the emotions are the clothing the heart wears: they express its preferences, its values, and its convictions.

In the rest of this chapter, we want to briefly look at a number of issues that may create emotional difficulties.

Attitudes Can Create Emotional Difficulties

In reports of great forest fires, you may run across the words, "A wind sprang up." Why should wind—the last thing anyone wants in the case of a fire—spring up at such a critical time? Because the fire itself created the wind. The rising heat caused an upward draft, drawing in more wind. In turn, the wind fed the fire, and the fire burned hotter and hotter.

In the case of attitudes and emotions, which is the fire? and which is the wind? You figure that out. One thing we know—attitudes feed emotions, and emotions feed attitudes. When the two get out of control and go in the wrong direction, it often ends up in a barrage of angry words. The words feed the flame. As the situation heats up, words flow faster and more furiously. The aftermath is like a charred landscape, full of regrets and guilt and bitter feelings—all because someone did not see what attitudes can do. No wonder James 3 tells us the tongue is like a fire.

Negative attitudes may be suppressed for a time. However, they are like an underground coal mine fire. The town of Centralia in eastern Pennsylvania was a typical coal-mining town with houses, churches, and stores. A large coal mine stretched under the town. One day this mine caught fire, and the workers were unable to put it out. It raged on, uncontrolled but out of sight, until it started creeping up through the ground. Today, there is hardly anything left of the town. Instead of seeing streets, buildings, and people, a motorist passing by sees smoking, sunken cavities, which give an eerie feeling that it is not over yet.

Similarly, our attitudes can turn us into a mental disaster area. Impressions and feelings, almost unconsciously, can lodge themselves deeply in our minds and inflict searing pain on our thoughts and outlook. Eventually these smoldering thoughts will flame forth, revealing that the soul has had its life burned out. Such thoughts need to be identified and dealt with if we hope to have freedom in the Lord.

On the positive side, good attitudes boost the emotions tremendously. When we feel as we ought on the inside, it is not as hard to feel good on the outside. The two help each other. That is why we are interested in preventing and avoiding the pitfalls of negative attitudes that drag down our emotions. We want to live on higher ground!

Emotional Struggles May Be Faith Issues

Emotions such as doubt, distrust, and discouragement are not pleasant. They rob us of the things we want most in life. They cloud the skies and crowd out the ability to see the good. What are the causes of such emotions?

Sometimes these struggles may result from a lack of faith in God. We may not have grasped the great truths about God's love and His faithfulness to the promises He gave to us.

Faith comes more easily for some people than for others. To them, it seems natural to believe who God is and what He says and what He does. For others, it seems more natural to question Him, even though they want to believe. They need to employ deliberate acts of the will to take God at His Word and to yield to it.

Some people struggle honestly in their effort to have faith. Sometimes their emotions cannot accept what the mind believes by faith. They doubt because they can't feel it. And if they follow their feelings more than the facts, they are headed for trouble.

Faith is a primary necessity for emotional strength and freedom. However, it is not fair to blame lack of faith for every emotional struggle people have, because other factors may be involved.

Emotional Struggles May Be Spiritual Issues

Not all emotional struggles are the result of sin. There may be innocent causes for them. But emotional struggles do result from sin often enough that the possibility needs to be considered. Emotional difficulties can occur if we do not stay current in our relationship with God. If we do not bring our failures and sins to Him in repentance and faith, we do have a problem. No sky is so heavy as one clouded by guilt.

Before we conclude that our gloomy or fearful spells or our "bad nerves" are (or are not) caused by sin, we need to do some honest soul-searching. If we open our hearts and souls to God, He is faithful to reveal what is deep inside us. The Bible and the Holy Spirit must be the primary source of our information—not our feelings. If we have a problem sorting this out, we ought to seek spiritual, mature believers who can help us find the way.

Emotional Difficulties Can Be Physical

Emotional difficulties are not always caused by intangible or spiritual matters. Like the rest of the body, the emotions can become overstressed and dysfunctional because of overwork. This can easily be seen in a tired first-grader who goes to bed laughing and crying at the same time. We recognize it easily enough in children (and maybe in others), but we are slow to recognize it in ourselves. It is right to ask ourselves at times, "Why do I feel so blue or so cranky?" and hit upon the obvious answer: "I'm tired;

that's why." Of course, to do that fairly, we must get past the tendency of thinking that we feel this way because of the way others are acting. One observant person said he couldn't believe how grouchy other people were when he was tired!

Chemical and hormone imbalances can also affect our emotions. Therefore, we might need to seek medical help if we cannot get to the root of a problem. But first, we should do all we can to make sure our emotional struggles are not caused by physical problems that we can find answers for.

Sometimes it may seem hard to tell. In one case, a man went to his doctor for help for his emotional problems. The doctor felt he had spiritual problems and sent him to his spiritual leader. The spiritual leader sent him back to the doctor and told him to ask for pills, which the doctor provided. Who was right?

Doctors look for the simple, close-to-home causes too. There is a saying among them: "When you hear thundering hooves, look for the horses before you look for zebras." In our search to find a name for our problem, it is likely that we do not need to look for a rare cause and cure. The cause and cure may well be in plain sight.

God wants to help us through these vulnerable areas of life. He wants us to walk closely with Him so that He can be our strength and stay. Then, and only then, will we be able to experience the emotional freedom He wants us to have!

Chapter
Two

What Is Being Free?

"Ye shall be free indeed" (John 8:36).

Freedom! From the beginning of time, men and women have coveted freedom. Adam and Eve wanted the freedom to do what they pleased. Ever since, people have perpetuated the idea that freedom is doing whatever yields the most pleasure. More wars have been fought in the name of freedom than for any other reason. Courts are clogged with people who think their rights of freedom have been abused. Even criminals commit crimes in the name of their own freedom.

Obviously there are different kinds of freedoms—national, civil, social, religious. Are these the freedoms Jesus was talking about when He said, "Ye shall be free indeed"? No. He was speaking of a much higher, more personal freedom than any of these—a better freedom than man could ever have before He came.

Let us compare freedom in the practical world with the kind of freedom Jesus wants us to have.

External Freedoms in Society

No matter which type of freedom we talk about, freedom is not simply doing whatever you please. Freedom is fragile and conditional. Freedom can quickly turn into fear.

In October, 1969, people living in Montreal, Canada's then largest city, spent sixteen hours of anxious terror when its entire police and fire departments went on strike. At first people felt free! No police to worry about! They did not need to heed the traffic lights. They did not worry about getting caught for speeding. What fun, what freedom! One reporter called it "almost a carnival atmosphere." But it was short-lived.

It wasn't long until there were serious traffic accidents. Worse yet, people started looting. More than 150 stores were broken into, and over $500,000 worth of merchandise was stolen. Other people began to settle old scores with their antagonizers. Soon people were afraid to drive, afraid to go outside—afraid of their own freedom!

Was that freedom? Were the people free indeed? No! Even the "free" lawbreakers feared each other. What a relief when the police came back on duty! This incident illustrates that in society we have freedom only within the structure of law and order.

What happens in the home if people come and go as they wish, eat whenever they feel like it, and have no respect for each other? Before long, tension and conflict rise because individual freedoms collide with each other. Thus freedom comes only when there is agreement and respect for procedure.

If you were an employer, what kind of success would you have if your workers took the freedom to come and go as they wished and worked only as they felt? How long would you be in business with a "free" labor force like that?

What kind of school would you have if students came and went as they wished, paid attention as they were inclined, and studied as they felt? Who would want to be a teacher, or even a student, in such a school?

What about our personal lives? Would we be free if no one dared infringe on our rights and notions? Would our lives produce only good? Would we really be happy with ourselves? Would others want to live with us?

How does freedom work in the church community? Would there be peace and serenity if everyone decided for himself what was acceptable? Would that make the church a light for truth and righteousness and a beacon of hope in our needy society? Would such a church help sustain your faith and help you live as you ought?

It might seem like we have belabored the point—a rather elementary point at that. Let's not be too sure. Have you never seen people—adults—leaving their churches, destroying their families, and ruining themselves in the name of freedom?

Hopefully, these descriptions have persuaded you that every type of freedom must have some boundaries, in order to represent true freedom. When we understand that, it helps us to see why God imposes certain limits on us to make us truly free.

At the same time, the freedom the Lord gives transcends all other freedoms. The freedom we are looking for can survive repressive governments, stricken economies, prisons, sickrooms, and the darkest of moments. For the Giver of this freedom is greater than all these! He gives freedom to our hearts.

Internal Freedom—What Is It?

Internal freedom comes when our heart, soul, and mind are at peace—at peace with ourselves, and even more important, at peace with God because we are reconciled to Him through Jesus. When this is true, our conscience is satisfied that we are living sincerely before God. We feel open with God and our fellow men. We are free from the feelings of bitterness and those things that keep us from rejoicing in the Lord. We are able to enjoy both sunshine and rain.

When freedom reigns in the soul, we delight in joy and peace. Sometimes we feel this freedom strongly. At other times, it is just a ray in the darkness. Jesus saw that ray when He went to the cross. According to Hebrews 12, He saw "the joy that was set before him." This kind of joy and peace is not merely a good feeling; it also provides affirmation and inner fortitude. Nehemiah understood it when he told the people, "The joy of the LORD is your strength." Jesus meant the same thing when He said in John 15:11, "These things have I spoken unto you, that my joy might remain in you, and that your joy might be full." This same joy is available to us today.

Does that mean we must have all our problems solved and everything going well for us before we can have peace? Is there any hope of freedom of spirit before we have all that? Yes, if we meet God's conditions, we can always have inner peace. However, God has not promised us a trouble-free life in this world. In fact, the opposite is true. Jesus talked more about suffering and sacrificial service than about ease and prosperity. He Himself had outward hardship and great suffering. But in it all, He endured steadfastly and graciously. And He promised His disciples that He would give them His peace when they had trouble. On the very night before His death, He told them, "These things I have spoken unto you, that in me ye might have peace. In the world ye shall have tribulation: but be of good cheer; I have overcome the world" (John 16:33). We too can claim this promise, if we are His disciples.

Even though God has not promised us a trouble-free life, we can rest in the fact that He understands us and our problems far better than we do. He has promised to be our Comforter in all the circumstances of life!

The Composition of Inner Freedom

How can we have such inner freedom even in turbulent times? What is the secret? The secret of freedom is this—and this may well be the most important statement in this book—***freedom is the product of other things.*** Freedom is the result of taking God's way. Freedom is not an end in itself; it must never be our primary and exclusive goal. If it is, it becomes elusive indeed, and the search for it will enslave us. Sometimes I find something more quickly when I am not looking for it specifically. At other times, when I can't find a paper on my desk, the quickest way to find it is to set things in order—and the sought-after paper appears.

Here is another illustration. If you look into a cupboard for a cake, you might say that no cake is there. But if a baker opens the same cupboard, finds the right ingredients, mixes them into a batter, and bakes them, he will have a cake. Was the cake in the cupboard? Yes and no. No—when you see only the ingredients. But yes—when the right ingredients are mixed in the right proportions and baked into a cake.

Who is the baker in our experience? Who writes the recipe for freedom? Who controls the process of mixing the ingredients and baking the cake? Is it not the Lord? We must want a right relationship with Him more than anything else. If we deal with Him only on the basis of wanting freedom from guilt, we miss the heart of the matter and will likely try to take shortcuts in the process.

If freedom is the cake, the Lord is the baker. We are like little children around Him, bringing Him pans and spoons, getting our fingers into the ingredients, and sometimes standing on chairs to watch. We do not make the cake; He does, and we merely cooperate with Him.

Cooperate? There is a better word, an even stronger word, and this is the greatest paradox of all—***freedom comes by surrender!***

If we insist that we can be free only when we have our own way, we have fallen into the greatest deception of all time. Even if we got all we wanted, it would not satisfy our deepest longings. It would be like a cake that used soap powder instead of baking powder.

Freedom comes when we surrender our self-will, our preferences—everything—to God. When we ask for nothing, claim no rights of our own, and commit the outcome totally to God, we have nothing to protect, nothing to lose, and everything to gain. We can relax. We are free because we have turned everything over to Him.

This is more easily said than done. Even when we are surrendered to God, we will face complications that we do not always understand, because our emotional makeup gets in the way. That is why so much of this book will discuss particular difficulties and pitfalls.

Let's conclude by constructing a profile of a heart that has the freedom Jesus spoke of.

Characteristics of the Free

What characteristics can you see in people who are free? What are they like? Although many people experience these virtues occasionally, only the truly free have them consistently.

The free love freely. They love because they have experienced the love of God in their hearts! And His love begs to be given to others. Love is also a choice. The free do not love just when they feel like it, for they know, "He that loveth not knoweth not God; for God is love" (1 John 4:8).

The free are not afraid to be hurt. Giving love is a risk because it might not be received. In fact, sometimes people reject our love, and react against it, and return nothing but pain. Paul said, "The more abundantly I love you, the less I be loved." But in spite of that, he said, "I will very gladly spend and be spent for you" (2 Corinthians 12:15). The free dare to love because their love is greater than the fear of being hurt.

The free are not afraid to risk failure. Satisfaction in life does not depend on a person's reputation or on a flawless string of successes. The free dare to offer themselves to their Maker for whatever He wants to make of them. That was why Caleb at eighty-five years old could say, "Give me this mountain!" He was not afraid. To be free, we must be willing to give our best to what we do, and leave the rest up to God.

The free do not fear examination or exposure. You may have heard of the man who sent a prankster telegram to his friends, saying, "All is known!" and how they all fled town. People are not free if they have to look over their shoulders because of hidden sins. When the free find themselves in the wrong, they are quick to correct the matter.

As one of the free, we do not need to worry in the security-check lines at airports. Since we have nothing to hide, we can calmly look the security officers in the eye as they check us out. Nor do we need to worry about a tax audit, since we have not knowingly cheated anyone. We do not even need to fear radar while we drive, because we are within the law. We can even appreciate the efforts of highway patrolmen.

The free are free from guile. When Jesus saw Nathanael coming to Him, He said, "Behold an Israelite indeed, in whom is no guile!" Nathanael was not deceitful, artificial, or pretentious. He was a sincere, straight-forward kind of man, who was not suspicious or surmising. He was genuine. He was one of the free.

The free are good. The Bible tells us in Acts 11:24 that Barnabas was "a good man, and full of the Holy Ghost and of faith." You can turn a good man inside out and examine him from any angle and in any situation, and he will still be good.

Does *good* mean that Barnabas was perfect? No, but he had a good heart. It affected his attitude toward God and life. We may be sure that if he found anything in himself other than goodness, he wanted to change. That kind of attitude served him well.

The free are great in faith. The Bible tells us that Barnabas was "full of the Holy Ghost and of faith." A heart that trusts God is free from worry and anxiety. Faith that commits all to God has nothing to lose, nothing to hold onto for itself. Trusting everything to God gives a child-like freedom.

The free are glad. We are also told that Barnabas was glad when he found believers at Antioch. Gladness is a unique possession of the free. True gladness springs from meaningful things. Free people focus on the good. They rejoice in it. They thank God for it. Freedom and gladness often come and go together.

The free are guiltless, guileless, good, great in faith, glad—and we could add words like *generous* and *gracious*. These words speak of unselfishness and caring about others.

Is it realistic to think that all these virtues can be ours? Not if we expect to wake up some fine morning and discover that we have them all. But they can be ours if we follow the road to spiritual growth that God has planned for us. If we constantly surrender ourselves to Him and let Him be Lord of our lives, it can be as He said, "If the Son therefore shall make you free, ye shall be free indeed."

CHAPTER THREE

The Problem of Bondage

"Whosoever committeth sin is the servant of sin" (John 8:34).

Man's problem with bondage is like a wild animal in a cage. Recently we visited a small zoo that exhibited lions and tigers and various wild cats. Some of them seemed quite content to lie lazily in the sun. Others paced along the high wire-mesh fence, back and forth, back and forth, until it almost made us dizzy. They all had somehow gotten into bondage, and they would stay there until someone released them, because the fences were bigger and stronger than they.

That is how it is with the human race. We were brought into bondage when our first parents were lured into sin. The results were just as Jesus said in our caption verse: "Whosoever committeth sin is the servant of sin." And it has been like that ever since.

But that was not the original plan. God has always wanted man to be free. When He put Adam and Eve in charge of the Garden of Eden, He gave them a tremendous amount of freedom, with only one restriction. Everything on earth was free for them to enjoy except the tree of the knowledge of good and evil. God solemnly warned them of the consequences if they violated that restriction.

But that one restriction became a pivotal point in history. Eve fell for the idea that the fruit from that tree stood between her and greater freedom. Ever since, the forbidden has had a seductive appeal to the natural mind. Just today a man told me that as soon as you tell people they can't do something, it becomes the very thing they think they must do.

What Adam and Eve failed to realize was that God had restricted them from that tree because they would have greater freedom when they left it alone. Everything God restricts us from threatens our freedom. And everything God directs us to do is a way to enhance true freedom. If we could keep that fact straight, it would save us a lot of struggle and heartache!

Ever since Eve (and Adam) reached for greater freedom and lost it all, their sons and daughters (including us) have been born in bondage. Ever since that time, man has always wanted to be free—not just free physically, but free in spirit. He is desperate to feel that he is his own person and not accountable to anyone. The mysterious allurement for that kind of freedom has dragged many a person into deep trouble—and held him there in bondage.

Worse yet, we have an enemy (Satan) who delights in seeing man lose freedom. Satan has never relented in his determination to hold everyone he can in perpetual bondage. That is why the battle goes on and on.

The Battle for Inner Freedom

Although the heavy hand holding us down is Satan's, there is another enemy even closer who is in full allegiance with Satan himself. That is our own carnal nature. How we hate to admit it! Yet, while we bemoan the struggle, we can so easily overlook our part in the battle.

Why? Because our *own* nature is carnal. Ever since the Fall of our first parents, our human nature has conflicted with what God requires of us. Our old nature wants its own way as a result of Adam and Eve taking their own way, back there in the Garden of Eden. The desires and appetites of our flesh are not in harmony with God nor with what is good for us.

Can we analyze the carnal nature? What are its components? What does it consist of? How can we expect it to act and react? Here are some points to consider.

Self-love. These days, men teach that self-love and self-respect are synonymous, and therefore we should please ourselves first. Some even say it is the eleventh commandment—an extension of "love thy neighbour as thyself" with the emphasis on *thyself.* This kind of teaching should not surprise us, since the Bible tells us that "in the last days . . . men shall be lovers of their own selves" (2 Timothy 3:1, 2).

Self-love is just a new name and new clothes for old-fashioned selfishness. It is an excuse to pamper ourselves and give ourselves what we want before we need to think about anyone else.

Pride. Pride must be on the top of any pile. Satan, the first victim of pride, could not stand to be in second place. Pride believes that "second place is first loser." It thrives on propping self up and putting others down. It protects its turf tenaciously and viciously if necessary. Pride hates not having its own way. It hates being told it can't have what it wants. And if it is wounded, watch out!

Lies. Jesus told the Pharisees, "Ye are of your father the devil. . . . When he speaketh a lie, he speaketh of his own: for he is a liar, and the father of it" (John 8:44). We are susceptible to the devil's lies about our rights. But by nature, we are no better, for our flesh even lies about its needs—and we are apt to believe it. Remember how Esau sold his birthright to Jacob for a bit of food? "After all," Esau said, "I will die if I do not have this food, and then

I won't be around to get the birthright anyway." Sounds ridiculous, doesn't it. But our flesh will be just as demanding and persuasive if we listen to it.

Excuses. An excuse may be just a low-profile lie. We could call this the "Don't blame me; it's not my fault" syndrome. The blaming-someone-else excuse is as old as Adam and Eve (and as modern as we are!). Read Genesis 3 to see how Adam and Eve passed the blame to others. Our carnal nature does the same, wiggling out of everything we let it get away with.

What is our first inclination? If we forget something, it is easy for us to think that someone should have reminded us—as if it was their responsibility! It is so easy (and so disturbing) to see others do that sort of thing. But what about us? We find it so easy to say "But . . ." while we are figuring out our excuse, or to say, "If he had not done what he did, I would not have done what I did." "Look what you made me do" is what we think, even if we do not say it.

Excuses may seem to be beneath our dignity. So we give an explanation instead. But then someone says, "Your explanation is just an excuse!" Could he be right?

Fear. The carnal nature is afraid to open up, to be exposed. It fears the unknown. Usually it tries to keep its tracks covered. Why is it hard for a sinner to confess his wrongdoing? It's fear. Fear of what? He isn't always sure. One thing is sure: "Fear hath torment."

Revelation 21:8 gives a list of those who shall be cast into the lake of fire. First on the list is "the fearful." Why? A Greek word-study book says, "The word denotes cowardice and timidity and is never used in a good sense." The carnal nature may boast great things, but inwardly it is covering up what it really is like. One honest person said, "Outside I act big and tough, but inside I'm a scared little boy." Fear is afraid to face facts and therefore does not deal with its needs.

We could discuss other elements of the carnal nature, but these expose the problem of bondage that we must all deal with. Our destiny pivots on how we face this problem. We must be serious about it because the one who wants to hold us in bondage is serious. We can be glad God has answers for us.

The Effect on Our Emotions

How do emotions fit into all this?

Emotions are caught in the conflict because they express what is going on inside a person. They add feeling to what is in his heart. And what his heart is dwelling on is bound to show—many times it is not for the good. Also, feelings can quickly fan the flame of a fire that is threatening to burn out of control.

Emotions are caught between the inner reality and the conscience. This puts emotions under pressure. The conscience lets a person know when he is not doing as he ought. And his emotions also feel the touch of God's convicting Spirit. The psalmist told us how his emotions were touched, in Psalm 32:3, 4: "When I kept silence, my bones waxed old through my roaring all the day long. For day and night thy hand was heavy upon me: my moisture is turned into the drought of summer."

There is a sense in which our emotions are the meeting point of the conflict between God and Satan for our souls. Satan appeals to us through our carnal nature, the flesh, while God speaks to us through the conscience. Emotions are caught in between but are powerless in themselves to change anything. Finally, they will be governed by whom we choose to serve.

The Good News

The good news is that we can find freedom from the terrible bondage of the carnal nature. But we cannot deliver ourselves from that bondage. This is where freedom must begin. Freedom must come from a source greater than ourselves. That source is God, who in His Son Jesus Christ came to earth to expose the bondage of sin. He is the only one who can unlock our prison door.

The next chapters will discuss how God did it and what His plan is for us. As you glance ahead, your first reaction might be, "I know all this already." Maybe so. But a review might bring a helpful idea to light that you had not thought of for some time. Let's review the basics, just to make sure.

CHAPTER
FOUR

The Freedom Jesus Promised

*"And ye shall know the truth,
and the truth shall make you free" (John 8:32).*

"The truth shall make you free." Through the ages, God has always wanted man to obey Him and to experience freedom. Sadly, man often ignores this plea and follows Satan. While Satan pretends to offer freedom, his ways only grip us in cruel bondage. But God has made a way for man to be free.

Free! Not just a little freedom, because moments after Jesus had promised this freedom, He added, "Ye shall be free *indeed!*" Free from what? Free to be what? And how can we stay free? The search for answers to these questions is the driving force of this book. The answers hold the key to serious, satisfying, fruitful Christian living.

Jesus said, "The truth shall make you free" to certain listeners who believed in Him. But some of His listeners, who did not believe in Him, took insult. They retorted, "We . . . were never in bondage to any man" (verse 33). Obviously they did not understand the freedom Jesus was talking about. They thought only of physical bondage, not spiritual bondage.

It is still the same today. Many people do not understand or experience the spiritual freedom Jesus came to proclaim. They try to be free in other ways. They confuse true freedom with the counterfeit freedom Satan and the world promote.

From the very beginning of His ministry, Jesus underscored the virtues of the freedom He represented. In fact, it was the heart of His first public proclamation in His hometown, Nazareth. He said, "The Spirit of the Lord is upon me, because he hath anointed me to preach the gospel to the poor; he hath sent me to heal the brokenhearted, to preach deliverance to the captives, and recovering of sight to the blind, to set at liberty them that are bruised" (Luke 4:18).

Note the words "deliverance to the captives" and "to set at liberty." Ironically, many of the "captives" in His audience did not know they were captives, and were not interested in being "set at liberty." They rose up in wrath, thrust Him out of the city, and tried to cast Him over a local bluff. By so doing, they missed one of the most marvelous opportunities ever offered to man.

In the caption verse of this chapter, Jesus explained that the key to freedom is truth. It is not notions or whims or wishes of men. It is from God.

But, of course, the old question, "What is truth?" insists on coming up. God's truth has various sides that need examination.

Characteristics of the Truth

Truth is absolute, undisputable, and unchangeable. Majority opinion does not alter it. Some people still claim that the earth is flat and that the sun goes around the earth. That does not change the fact that the earth is round and orbits the sun. That is how God's truth is. It stands undaunted, whether it is accepted or rejected. Truth is reality. And it never bows to the fantasies and imaginations of men.

The patient consistency of truth provides powerful reassurance. Just as the guiding star waited for the wise men when they forsook it and made their detour into Jerusalem to find the babe Jesus, the truth is still waiting to be believed and received.

Here are some facts about truth that will help to set us free.

First, we must want to know the truth. God has given us the power of choice. If we don't sincerely want to know, we will stay in the dark. For instance, Pilate asked that immortal question in John 18:38. He said, "What is truth?" but the truth never did him any good because he did not ask with honest intent. It was simply an excuse.

Jesus attached further meaning to wanting to know the truth, in John 7:17, "If any man will do his will, he shall know of the doctrine, whether it be of God, or whether I speak of myself." He meant that to really know the truth, we must be ready to do what we know. Truth will set us free only if we obey it. Otherwise, it takes us into deeper bondage—the terrible state of deception!

Second, truth defines real bondage. By nature, man hates the thought of being in bondage. He refuses to admit he is in bondage and might even deny it vehemently. For instance, he may say he can quit smoking whenever he chooses, but discreetly avoid trying to quit lest he be proven wrong.

Satan capitalized on this mindset in his first attack on Eve. He led her to think that God was selfishly holding her and Adam hostage by not allowing them to eat of the tree of the knowledge of good and evil. Satan claimed that if they ate, they would be truly free. Eve fell for his trick. She wanted to get out of this supposed bondage. So she ate to find freedom—only to get the absolute opposite of what she wanted.

Sin is bondage. Jesus laid this out firmly when He said, "Verily, verily, I say unto you, Whosoever committeth sin is the servant of sin" (John 8:34). Paul confirmed the same thing in Romans 6:16: "Know ye not, that to whom ye yield yourselves servants to obey, his servants ye are to whom ye obey; whether of sin unto death, or of obedience unto righteousness?"

We need to accept this. We must acknowledge that we are hopelessly afflicted with sin and are helpless to deliver ourselves from this bondage. Even if we rid ourselves of certain sins by sheer willpower, we are still under the power of the sin nature and its unending demands for attention and satisfaction.

What is the answer? How can we be set free if willpower and self-discipline will not suffice? This problem can only be remedied by following the answer Paul discovered after he cried out, "O wretched man that I am! who shall deliver me from the body of this death? I thank God through Jesus Christ our Lord" (Romans 7:24, 25).

Paul described his delight in the law of God in verse 22. But then, in the midst of his noble desires, he confessed, "But I see another law in my members, warring against the law of my mind, and bringing me into captivity to the law of sin which is in my members" (verse 23). He finally realized that he could never, ever deliver himself from this bondage.

What was true of Paul is true of us. We can never free ourselves. We can never become good enough or strong enough to deliver ourselves by our own strength.

Third, truth details the plan of salvation. God has provided an answer to the deadly plight in which humanity finds itself. The bars of sin have been torn away, and there is hope for the captives.

God was not slow in responding to the bondage into which Adam and Eve fell. Even while pronouncing His sentence on them and on the serpent, who caused it all, He promised that there would be a Redeemer—that He would provide a way to find victory over the awful power of sin.

"And I will put enmity between thee and the woman, and between thy seed and her seed; it shall bruise thy head, and thou shalt bruise his heel" (Genesis 3:15).

Ever since the Fall, the serpent has bruised the heel of humanity. But God promised that there was a day coming when the seed of the woman would bruise the serpent's head by breaking his power over the human race and setting men and women free to live for Him. That day came when Jesus came!

The prophets kept alive the promise of the coming freedom. John the Baptist proclaimed it, and Jesus picked it up aggressively. He said it in many different ways. Once He drew a parallel from Jewish history: "And as Moses lifted up the serpent in the wilderness, even so must the Son of man be lifted up: that whosoever believeth in him should not perish, but have eternal life" (John 3:14, 15).

Then He said what became the golden text of the Bible, in John 3:16, "For God so loved the world, that he gave his only begotten Son, that whosoever believeth in him should not perish, but have everlasting life."

And what would this freedom be like? Would it be mere survival, a last-gasp kind of life? We will let the Master speak for Himself.

"In the last day, that great day of the feast, Jesus stood and cried, saying, If any man thirst, let him come unto me, and drink. He that believeth on me, as the scripture hath said, out of his belly shall flow rivers of living water" (John 7:37, 38).

"I am the door: by me if any man enter in, he shall be saved, and shall go in and out, and find pasture. . . . I am come that they might have life, and that they might have it more abundantly" (John 10:9, 10).

Obviously Jesus was speaking of Himself. He was inviting all to the fountain of living water, the one He talked about to the Samaritan woman at the well. "But whosoever drinketh of the water that I shall give him shall never thirst; but the water that I shall give him shall be in him a well of water springing up into everlasting life" (John 4:14).

No wonder the woman said, "Sir, give me this water, that I thirst not."

Another time, when Jesus used bread to teach the same lesson, His listeners requested, "Lord, evermore give us this bread" (John 6:34).

Jesus is the author of true freedom. He is the only way to freedom for us. He put the promise, the plan, and the provision in place. Now, who can have it?

Fourth, truth has conditions. Obviously, freedom is not forced on anyone. In fact, the conditions are such that the casual observer may go away thinking it is actually bondage rather than freedom! What a pity.

Condition #1: Believe in Jesus. "Then said Jesus to those Jews which *believed* on him, . . . " They believed what He told them, not only about freedom, but about everything else. They believed what He told them about Himself—that truly He was the Messiah, the Son of God who had come to save them.

Condition #2: Acknowledge that you are indeed in spiritual bondage. You need to admit you are a servant of sin and that you are helpless to escape its clutches. You cannot excuse yourself or shift the blame. Freedom is only for those who accept responsibility for their condition.

Condition #3: Become a disciple (follower) of the Lord Jesus Christ. He is the only one who is stronger than the devil, who is holding you captive in sin. Only by absolute loyalty to Christ in attitude and in action can you find freedom. Accept His direction and discipline. Make His Word the law of your life. This, in summary, is the mystery revealed: True freedom comes by accepting the way of another, the way of our Lord Jesus Christ!

Condition #4: Continue in this way. Jesus put it very simply, even bluntly: "If ye continue in my word, then are ye my disciples indeed; and ye shall know the truth, and the truth shall make you free" (John 8:31, 32).

In summary, the truth is so simple that many stumble over it. Nevertheless, we must believe it, embrace it, and live by it continually. This is God's formula for freedom. There are no substitutes or shortcuts. And there is no way to really understand it without experiencing it!

CHAPTER FIVE

The Freedom Jesus Provided

"If the Son therefore shall make you free, ye shall be free indeed" (John 8:36).

This chapter focuses on what it cost God to provide freedom—spiritual freedom, which is the basis of emotional freedom. It should help us to grasp the magnitude of what Jesus suffered to set us free.

We can appreciate our freedom only to the extent that we understand the price of it. That is why history books emphasize how men in the past struggled and sacrificed to liberate their people. The cost of our spiritual freedom has never been equaled, and the quality of the freedom has never been matched.

The Price of Our Freedom

First, Jesus had to take on a human body. We are told that before He came to earth, He was "equal with God" (Philippians 2:6). But when He was incarnated on the earth, He "made himself of no reputation, and took upon him the form of a servant, and was made in the likeness of men" (Philippians 2:7). Thereby He was called the Son of Man.

Hebrews 2:9 describes further what took place. "But we see Jesus, who was made a little lower than the angels." Why? "For the suffering of death." The price of our freedom was the sacrificial death of a perfect man. Since there was no perfect man, God Himself had to take on a human body. This God-man, this Son, had to live a perfect life and then offer up His body and perfect blood as the sacrifice for the sin of the whole world. This is the heart and life of the Gospel.

Hebrews 9:14 sums up Christ's great work like this: "How much more shall the blood of Christ, who through the eternal Spirit offered himself without spot to God, purge your conscience from dead works to serve the living God?" That is why Jesus could say without apology and hesitation that "If the Son therefore shall make you free, ye shall be free indeed."

For freedom to become reality, Jesus had to be more than just a Saviour. His work on Calvary was not the last chapter in providing freedom for us. In fact, it was only the beginning of His work in our behalf. We must experience the whole Jesus, everything He is, in order to be truly free.

The Person of Our Emancipator

First, Jesus became the go-between, a bridge between God and man. He was the answer to the needs of mankind throughout the Old Testament. Job's heart cried out, "Neither is there any daysman betwixt us, that might lay his hand upon us both" (Job 9:33).

Jesus was the only one who could be the daysman. By fulfilling the Old Testament, He confirmed His authority to be the testator of a new covenant, which is recorded in the New Testament. Hebrews 9:15 assures us of the power of His death by saying, "For this cause he is the mediator of the new testament."

To be our mediator, Jesus had to meet the approval of our righteous, holy God as well as meet the needs of sinful humanity. In so doing, He became our high priest and our intercessor—our advocate for all our needs before the righteous God. He is far more than a political lobbyist in heaven on behalf of humans. He is credible to both God and man and has cleared a path between the two.

"Wherefore in all things it behoved him to be made like unto his brethren, that he might be a merciful and faithful high priest in things pertaining to God, to make reconciliation for the sins of the people. For in that he himself hath suffered being tempted, he is able to succour them that are tempted" (Hebrews 2:17, 18).

Several chapters later, in Hebrews 7:25, God offers one of the greatest imaginable assurances: "Wherefore he is able also to save them to the uttermost that come unto God by him, seeing he ever liveth to make intercession for them."

Freedom comes by well-grounded confidence. It comes by knowing that Jesus is a credible representative in our behalf. We do not have the responsibility of settling our account with God by ourselves. Our only responsibility is to have a genuine relationship with Jesus so that we can have the benefit of His death on the cross for us.

Where is our advocate, our go-between? Is He far away? On the one hand, we are told in Hebrews 9:24 that He has entered "into heaven itself, now to appear in the presence of God for us." On the other hand, he is much closer to us than that!

Jesus not only dwells in heaven—He also dwells in His children. He enters into a partnership with those who believe and open their hearts to Him. Indeed, He bears the greater part of the burden for making this relationship work. Hear His invitation in Matthew 11:28–30: "Come unto me, all ye that labour and are heavy laden, and I will give you rest. Take my yoke upon you, and learn of me; for

I am meek and lowly in heart: and ye shall find rest unto your souls. For my yoke is easy, and my burden is light."

Just how can He—how *does* He—do it? That's the mystery of the ages, the mystery of the Gospel, referred to in Colossians 1:27: "To whom God would make known what is the riches of the glory of this mystery among the Gentiles; which is Christ in you, the hope of glory."

"Christ in you"! Think about it. This is the secret and source of the freedom Christ offers to us. It is His divine presence and power in us that sets us free from sin, because where Christ is, sin cannot dwell or be in control. Truly, this is our hope for both present and future glory.

The apostles received the Spirit of Christ on Pentecost. It made such a difference in their lives that they completely baffled the scribes and rulers who tried to deal with them. The Bible tells us in Acts 4 that the rulers called them in to try to stop their powerful preaching. "Now when they saw the boldness of Peter and John, and perceived that they were unlearned and ignorant men, they marvelled; and they took knowledge of them, that they had been with Jesus."

Been with Jesus? What the scribes and rulers did not know was that not only had they been with Jesus—He now dwelt in them!

The key to freedom is still the same. Jesus, through the Holy Spirit, dwells in His own. God tells us how it works, in 2 Corinthians 3:17, "Now the Lord is that Spirit: and where the Spirit of the Lord is, there is liberty." That is freedom.

Through Jesus Christ we can obtain the marvelous gift of freedom that God offers to all. Freedom from the guilt of sin. Freedom from the power of sin. Freedom by His presence within. Freedom to live.

The last verse of 2 Corinthians 3 tells us how it is to work: "But we all, with open face beholding as in a glass the glory of the Lord, are changed into the same image from glory to glory even as by the Spirit of the Lord."

Just before Jesus went to the cross, He gave some insights concerning how deep He wanted this freedom to reach. He said in John 14:1, "Let not your heart be troubled." He came to give us freedom from our vexed, troubled hearts. He wants to be our answer to life's fears and frustrations. His closing admonition to them was, "These things I have spoken unto you, that in me ye might have peace. In the world ye shall have tribulation: but be of good cheer; I have overcome the world" (John 16:33).

And then, just before He went back to the Father in heaven, He promised, "I am with you alway, even unto the end of the world. Amen" (Matthew 28:20). The Son is on our side—or better yet—He has brought us onto His side. Where the Son is, there is freedom!

"If the Son therefore shall make you free, ye shall be free indeed."

Chapter Six

Being Free Indeed

"Ye shall be free INDEED" (John 8:36).

A man was plodding along the road, carrying a heavy pack on his back. A kind man with a horse and wagon came along and offered him a ride. Gratefully he accepted and climbed on.

Shortly the driver turned and saw that his passenger was still clutching his heavy pack. "Why don't you set the pack down?" he said. "You don't need to hold it."

"Oh," said the passenger, "you have been so kind in letting me ride that I don't want to bother you with my pack too."

We could say, "How silly! Didn't he know the weight was on the wagon?" He was carrying a load he did not need to carry. He could not enjoy his ride to the fullest.

The Emotional Realization

Our emotions can be like the man riding on the wagon. They may not have grasped what the heart has accepted by faith. They still carry the burden of past guilt and have not become aware of the new privileges a child of God may enjoy. The emotions may be misinformed or may have become so skeptical, that salvation from sin sounds too good to be true. The head may grasp facts about salvation that one's feelings have not yet fully comprehended.

Our emotions are not a predictable guide. They can be like a dog zigzagging around his master, who is walking along a straight path. Sometimes our emotions take us where we do not want to go, and sometimes they keep us from going where we should go. To benefit fully from our emotions, it is extremely important that they are turned in the right direction.

Freedom of the soul—or at least the *feeling* of that freedom—can be elusive. While the "feeling" side of our relationship with God is not primary, it does influence us deeply. In fact, the liberated soul who still feels imprisoned often finds that his salvation is eclipsed by his feelings.

We can be like Peter when he was in prison. Acts 12 tells us how he went to sleep that night, securely chained between two soldiers in the highest security department of the prison. Suddenly there was a light, and he was awakened abruptly. Robotlike, he followed orders, went through the prison gates, and finally found himself alone on the street. He thought he was dreaming, but in truth, an angel had liberated him. He was free and didn't know it. Eventually he came to himself and was on his way. Meanwhile, imagine his confusion!

There is a similar story about a farmer who brought a small flock of quail to the Indian village market. He had tied a string around one foot of each bird and tied all the strings to a ring on a central stick. The quail walked dolefully around and around, like mules turning a millstone. Nobody seemed to pity them until a devout Hindu felt sorry for the poor creatures. He inquired the price and said, "I'll buy them all." The farmer was elated and gratefully accepted the money.

"Now," the buyer said, "I want you to set them free."

"What was that?" the puzzled farmer exclaimed.

"You heard me. Cut them loose, and set them free."

"Well, all right." So saying, he severed the strings and set the birds free. What happened? The quail simply kept on marching around and around in the same circle. Finally, he had to scare them into flight. Even when they landed some distance away, they resumed marching. Free, unbound, released, yet going around in circles as if still tied.

Perhaps we have been indeed set free from the guilt of our sins, but our emotions have not comprehended the reality. Our emotions would keep us lying in a prison cell, totally unaware that the door is unlocked and waiting for us to pass through, unaware that the strings of guilt and bondage have been cut!

This brings us back to the last word of our caption verse: *indeed*. Free indeed—not just technically or judicially free, but free in reality. Not just partially free, but free to live life to its fullest. Jesus chose this word because *indeed* means to be truly, actually, really free. And this can hardly happen until the soul has grasped the marvel of it all.

The slaves of the Deep South demonstrated this vividly. President Abraham Lincoln had declared them free; they were judicially free. But for some former slaves, it was frightening. For generations, all the decisions had been made for them. Whatever they had, someone had given them. They had no say in their destiny.

Suddenly it was all different. They could pack whatever meager possessions they had, wave good-bye disdainfully to their old masters, and be gone. Some of them did just that. But some found out that the world was much bigger and crueler than they had imagined, even crueler than their old master. Ere long they were worse off than they had been at home on the plantation. Some went back to where they had come from and willingly traded their so-called freedom for the meager security of their former bondage!

Then there were those who did not know they were free. They could not read, so if no one told them, they were in the dark. (Their masters probably were not eager to tell them.) Judicially they were free, but they did not know it. Hence their freedom did them no good.

Some slaves may even have thought their freedom allowed them the opportunity to take revenge on their former masters. They may have felt that their freedom gave them the right to bypass law and order. This idea of freedom would have brought them worse trouble than their slavery ever did.

Likewise, some people seem to think that freedom in Christ gives them an opportunity to live as they please, without guilt—that God has given them free pardon for their failure to uphold His laws. But this does not free them from carnal bondage. In reality, God set us free from the lower laws of the flesh by enabling us to live by His higher law of noble love and liberty.

A Picture of an Imprisoned Soul

While David was running from King Saul, he hid in a cave for safety. From this cave, he penned a prayer, likening his soul's condition to that of his physical situation, living in a cave prison. He said, in Psalm 142:7, "Bring my soul out of prison." What was his problem? What was holding him captive? Why wasn't he free? Why did he feel that his soul was in prison?

We get a hint of the answer in the words he added, "That I may praise thy name." Apparently he wanted to praise the Lord, but his soul was hemmed in by his other problems. He could not praise the Lord when his soul was in prison.

David wrote down how he felt. He cried and poured out his complaint. His spirit was overwhelmed by his troubles. Everywhere he went, his enemy had laid a snare for him. He felt horribly alone. No one even wanted to know him. His persecutors were stronger than he was.

No wonder he was in the depth of despair. It is a wonder he even wanted to be delivered. Why didn't he just roll over and die? Apparently, he believed there was a way out, and he knew he wanted something better.

Were the things he was saying really true, or were they mere illusions? Were things as dark and dreadful as he thought they were? Suppose we had been there with him in the cave prison while King Saul hunted him like a partridge. How would it have seemed to us? Remember too that he did not have the luxury of knowing how things would work out.

Apparently David understood that a man could be in a physical prison and yet be free in soul and spirit. In his soul prison, it was dark and dismal. There was nothing but uncertainty and fear. He could not see a glimmer of hope, and there was nothing there to cheer him. Yet he must have believed that it was possible to rise above the worst of circumstances and still rejoice. That was why he prayed to be delivered from soul prison.

The greatest monster that grips the soul is sin. It fastens its stranglehold on its victims and is loath to let go. But sin is not always the problem. It was not necessarily David's problem in this case. Even after someone has been delivered from sin, Satan never gives up trying to throw a mantle of darkness over him in some way or other. This matter is one of the core problems we must all deal with.

How did David find his way out of soul prison?

The Path to True Freedom

Dark as it was in the prison, David did one right thing. He turned to God. Whether it was the last resort or not, he did it. He prayed. He confessed his need. He stated his desire.

The next psalm (143) was probably written about a different situation (when David fled from Absalom), yet it fits well into our discussion here. Again, David wrote his feelings of desolation and the need of his own soul. He said his spirit was overwhelmed and his heart was distressed.

Then something significant happened: he remembered. He started looking back, and good memories started coming. And it seems the longer he remembered, the faster his good memories came—maybe even faster than his troubles had come!

That was the turning point. Instead of thinking about his troubles, he started to meditate on God's work in his life. He stretched his hands and thirsty soul to God. "Hear me speedily," he cried. "In thee do I trust." He pled for deliverance, he asked to be taught, he asked to be quickened.

Last but not least, he pledged himself to God, saying, "I am thy servant." No strings attached, no favors demanded, just an unconditional commitment to the God so freshly revealed to him. And how did he receive this revelation of God? By remembering, meditating, and following on.

Did God hear David? Did God deliver his soul from prison? Was he again able to praise the Name of the Lord? Evidently he was, because his triumph spills out in other psalms of praise.

Does that sound too easy? How can we have such freedom under difficult circumstances? In later chapters, we will discuss various difficulties. Here, however, we will let the apostle Peter give us some help.

Peter's writings concentrated on rejoicing in the midst of suffering. He knew that believers can experience a level of freedom that even persecution cannot destroy. Here are a few of his statements.

"That the trial of your faith, being much more precious than of gold that perisheth, though it be tried with fire, might be found unto praise and honour and glory at the appearing of Jesus Christ: whom having not seen, ye love; in whom, though now ye see him not, yet believing, ye rejoice with joy unspeakable and full of glory: receiving the end of your faith, even the salvation of your souls" (1 Peter 1:7–9).

"Beloved, think it not strange concerning the fiery trial which is to try you, as though some strange thing happened unto you: but rejoice, inasmuch as ye are partakers of Christ's sufferings; that, when his glory shall be revealed, ye may be glad also with exceeding joy" (1 Peter 4:12, 13).

This was true not only for the twelve apostles, but also for many Christians since that time, who have suffered horribly, but victoriously, for the Lord Jesus Christ. *Martyrs Mirror* gives many accounts of saints going to their death with a testimony of peace and joy.

Many other Scriptures point to the freedom we receive by being willing to suffer and even to relinquish our physical lives. The soul whose only goal is to be in the will of God is free because he has committed all to his Maker and Keeper.

We want to move on now to discuss more closely some of the practical aspects of emotional freedom.

Chapter Seven

Freedom and the Emotions

In this chapter we will discuss how our emotions affect us in general, and how they can affect our freedom in the Lord. God wants His freedom to affect and stabilize our emotions in daily life.

Our emotions are not an end in themselves. They are not to be the final authority in our lives. While they are influential and powerful, God does not intend that they override one's will and better judgment.

Emotions are a gift from God. Without them, we could only see life as if we were paging through a picture book, seeing winter scenes but not shivering, seeing desert photos but never panting with thirst. Having no emotions might be comfortable, in a way, but it would also be a very detached existence. How unfortunate the man who never felt sorrow, happiness, thankfulness, or deep indebtedness to someone!

Valuable as they are, emotions are delicate and vulnerable. If they get out of balance, they can rob us of our peace and joy. As we go along, we want to discuss some common struggles and give practical suggestions to help us enjoy the blessings God intended for us to have through our emotions.

God has given different individuals different degrees of emotional intensity. Some people's feelings rise to the surface quickly and urgently. They can have six emergencies in one morning! Other people hardly seem to feel at all—as if they have thicker skin.

Our own emotions may vary from time to time. One time we may feel one way and another time another way—almost like a different person. How should we feel about the way we feel? When are we emotionally free, and when are we not? Does God have a plan flexible enough to fit our emotional makeup? Let's consider what God's intentions were when He gave us emotions.

The Purpose for Emotions

Emotions help us choose right. God made us creatures of choice. We must choose between right and wrong, between God and Satan, between heaven and hell. We must make difficult choices that require strong resolution. God gave us emotions so we could make these decisions not only with our heads but also with our hearts.

Maybe some people can make right decisions strictly from cool calculations. Maybe they know about the love of God and the hatred of Satan and the beauty of heaven and the horrors of hell intellectually in their minds. But could you really understand all this without a measure of feeling? God gave us the bonus of feelings to confirm and encourage active faith.

Emotions give us a sense of urgency. "It needs to be done," our emotions say. "Do it now." Once we follow a task through to completion, our emotions give us a sense of satisfaction.

Emotions help us to have pleasure in life. For example, think of food. God could have made all food taste like sand or sawdust. But He gave it delightful flavor. Did He do it because the value of the food is in the flavor? I am no expert on food, but I doubt it. God gave flavor to food so we could enjoy it. It makes the basic necessity of eating pleasurable.

Perhaps the psalmist had something similar in mind when he said, in Psalm 34:8, "O taste and see that the LORD is good: blessed is the man that trusteth in him." Peter put it similarly in 1 Peter 2:3: "If so be ye have tasted that the Lord is gracious."

Taste means more than a mere nibble. It means to eat, experience, and enjoy! Emotions help us to feel the goodness of God. They confirm what we know by faith.

Experience affirms that responding to the goodness of God and everything else He is to us gives us great pleasure. Our emotions do not produce that pleasure—they simply confirm and echo it.

Did you know that God has pleasure too? Leviticus and Numbers say dozens of times that the offerings God's people brought Him were a "sweet savour." They were delightful and very pleasant to Him! Add this from Psalm 149: "The LORD taketh pleasure in his people."

Emotions help us to find refreshment. Emotions help the soul to rest. Jesus said, "Come unto me, all ye that labour and are heavy laden, and I will give you rest." We can feel when our souls are at rest. Our emotions are rejuvenated when we rest in the Lord by taking our burdens to Him and leaving them there.

The emotions also affect the body's ability to rest. It is difficult for the body to slow down if the emotions are running hard. But if they are relaxed, the body can enjoy repose. Ecclesiastes 5:12 tells us, "The sleep of a labouring man is sweet."

Emotions help us to fear. Fear may seem like an unpleasant feeling. And it can get out of hand. But imagine a child who does not fear fire or water. Or imagine a vehicle driver who has no fear. Such a driver usually terrorizes others because he is not safe to ride with.

Fear helps us to be cautious and to take preventive measures. It encourages keeping a margin of safety rather than being foolhardy. It makes us aware that we are vulnerable and destructible. God uses it to sharpen our self-preservation instincts.

But God has a higher reason to give us the emotion of fear. He wants to teach us to fear Him—and then in turn, to fear sin and evil. Those whose slogan is "No Fear" will one day wish they had feared the right things.

Emotions help us to grieve. Expressing grief through the emotions gives release to the burdened soul. It is like draining a wound. It enables us to find healing. More than that, the ability to express grief can help us sympathize with others and comfort those who are hurting.

Not expressing grief is akin to being locked up in a dungeon. Those who face the pain or death of loved ones without expressing any emotion often find themselves locked up in a cold, stony prison of emotional pain. By stifling their sad emotions, they stifle their glad ones too.

Our emotions are to be like amiable friends. They are given to us to make our life journey pleasant and profitable. For that to work, they need to be kept in their proper place within God's divine plan. And that is not always easy.

The Power of Emotions

It was late afternoon in a rural village. The fire siren wailed. Volunteer firemen rushed to their pickups. Watching them roar up the road to the fire station, someone remarked, "One of those men just came home from work and said, 'I'm so tired I can't go another step.' Look at him go now!" The observer meant that a sudden emotion can stir up even a weary man.

Our emotions can make a work assignment look like a welcome challenge or like a formidable giant. They can show us the problem, or they can show us the pleasure of a task. They can fasten our eyes on the lofty mountain peaks of freedom or trap us in dark valleys of despair. If our emotions are running high, nothing looks impossible. If they are running low, nothing looks possible. We know that grave danger lies on either end of that pendulum swing.

The power of emotions makes them deceitful. They make us feel different depending on what time of day it is. Did you ever notice how different your work looks in the morning compared with how it looks in the evening when you are tired? That can be confusing to us as well as to those around us. As with an undependable clock, we must double-check our emotions against the facts lest they deceive us.

Our emotions can easily become our master rather than our servant. They can become so strong that they affect our thinking patterns and drown out our common sense. If let go, they can even break down our willpower, and that means trouble. We dare not discredit or ignore the power of our emotions.

Problems Emotions Create

It is no surprise that our feelings can create problems. With their ready access to our thinking, they are like lobbyists among the lawmakers—always clamoring for what they want! Or they are like children who have learned to get what they want by continual begging.

Emotions may be influenced. Some people decide how they ought to feel and then go ahead and feel that way. They are a rare breed. Other people allow their emotions to tell them what to think and just follow them wherever they lead.

Probably most of us are somewhere in between these two extremes. However, our emotions are still influenced by our own set of core values. They know what we are receptive to and what we won't listen to. In that way, they are like a shoe salesman who keeps offering us this and that until we buy. Our emotions are constantly testing the fringes of our tolerance and cooperation. In areas where we are weak, our emotions will take over. For instance, if anger is our weakness, anger will be a strong emotion.

Our emotions are influenced by the people we are with. Everyone is emotional, and other people's emotions touch ours. That is why the Bible gives strong direction about whom we associate with, which church we join, and whom we marry.

Let's note several examples of how groups of people affected each other. A week before Jesus was crucified, the crowds adoringly threw their garments before Him in His triumphal entry into Jerusalem. A week later, the mob cried for His crucifixion. It is a safe guess that some people were part of both crowds. They followed the prevailing opinion both times.

Sometimes emotions fuel a mob spirit. This happened at Ephesus after the Christians there turned away from idols. The hucksters were infuriated and incited a riot. Acts 19:32 gives us a graphic summary: "Some therefore cried one thing, and some another: for the assembly was confused; and the more part knew not wherefore they were come together." Believe it or not, our emotions can take us in that direction as well.

Our emotions are influenced by circumstances. It is usually not so hard to be happy if everything is going our way. But a flat tire, a burnt meal, a rebuke, or a cutting remark can send our feelings plummeting. Remember Haman, who was extremely elated because the king paid attention to him, but then was extremely upset over one man who refused to bow to him.

Our feelings toward others can change dramatically, depending on what they last said or did to us. The problem is that these signals are not dependable, because those people are subject to changeable emotions too.

Our emotions can take radical mood swings. As the little chorus goes, "You find it easy to pray and to sing all the day / When your cup runneth over with joy." *But* "You find it easy to doubt and to cry and to pout / When your cup is all empty and dry."

Take the example of Elijah. First Kings 18 gives the account of his contest with King Ahab and all the prophets of Baal to demonstrate who is God. Four hundred fifty prophets came to represent Baal, but Elijah alone stood for God. Undaunted, he prayed, and God sent fire down from heaven. By the time his sacrifice and the altar were consumed, and the barrels of water he had dumped over it were all licked up by the fire, the crowd around him was ready to slay the four hundred fifty false prophets. What a victory!

But the very next day, Queen Jezebel sent word to him that by the following day he would be a dead man. Instead of facing that threat as he had faced her prophets, Elijah fled for his life. First Kings 19:4 shows how he felt: "He himself went a day's journey into the wilderness, and came and sat down under a juniper tree: and he requested for himself that he might die; and said, It is enough; now,

O LORD, take away my life; for I am not better than my fathers."

What had happened? How had he gone from boldly facing four hundred fifty screaming false prophets to running from one woman? Furthermore, did he really want to die? That's debatable, because Jezebel had declared she was ready to help him!

Jonah is another illustration of how the emotions can vacillate. When he was finally ready to go preach in Nineveh, he boldly traversed the city, declaring, "Yet forty days, and Nineveh shall be overthrown." The people—even the king—listened and repented. To the bewilderment of any evangelist who reads this today, Jonah was not happy about that. On a hill outside Nineveh, he prayed, "Therefore now, O LORD, take, I beseech thee, my life from me; for it is better for me to die than to live" (Jonah 4:3). He seemed insulted that the doom he preached didn't happen. He had a problem appreciating the mercy of God!

From our viewpoint, we might ask, "How could these two men change like that?" Apparently they were victimized by their own feelings. Somehow they lost sight of what was really important.

Emotions can be affected by weariness. This may have been part of Elijah's problem in the wilderness. His mountaintop experience may have worn him out. Weariness can magnify problems and dangers to the point where we despair of facing them. On the other hand, weariness can take away our sense of danger. That is why it is dangerous to drive when we are sleepy. That is also why we should avoid making decisions when we are tired.

Our emotions might lie to us. Deliberately? Probably not. But that is just the problem. Our emotions tend to believe our feelings rather than the facts—and feelings are very persuasive.

Did you ever observe a dispute between two teams of children on a playground? Did everyone on one team see clearly that Frank was out, and did everyone on the other team see clearly that he was safe? Maybe nobody was lying, but each team's emotions led them to believe what they wanted to believe. Too often, what we see fits what we prefer. In fact, someone has said that the emotions lie more often than they tell the truth. Is that true? Maybe not totally, but at least it provides food for thought.

Our emotions tend to justify our wrong feelings or wrong doings. They are not bashful about saying we have a right to feel the way we do because of the way we have been treated. When someone challenges us about our attitude, we are quick to defend ourselves.

However, our emotions can misinterpret how others treat us. They can turn a kindness someone intended to do to us into an offense. They may tell us others are watching us critically when they are only concerned and interested in us.

Common Questions

How can I know if my emotions are taking me for a ride? How can I know if they are trustworthy? What if I begin to wonder who I really am because of how often my emotions swing from one side to the other? Some of these questions may seem very important at the moment; but as time goes by, we may look back and smile (or wince) at how we felt.

And here are some questions that are often asked regarding the spiritual side of our emotional state.

If I am not happy, is something wrong? My relationship with the Lord seems flat, and I don't feel assured of His approval. Right now it is hard to feel good about anything. Is this a sure sign that there is sin somewhere?

If God does not seem near, has He left me? Has He written me off as a hopeless case? When I read my Bible and pray, nothing happens. It seems like a waste of time. What does that mean?

Are the feelings I struggle with really wrong? When I swing up and down emotionally, does my relationship with God go with it?

What can I do when I have tried everything I know and everything others have told me? The Lord knows how I have struggled, but I am still at the same spot and don't seem to make much progress.

Why can't I just do whatever it takes and be forever delivered from my emotional struggles? Why do I end up doing the same things over and over? Why, why?

Can you identify with any of this? Maybe these kinds of questions don't bother you. Maybe some very clear answers rushed through your mind—especially for someone else! Perhaps you felt like saying, "How can you be so 'heathen' as to feel like that? Don't you know . . . ?"

You might say, as someone did to me, "Discouraged? I don't even remember the last time I felt that way." Regardless of how true that might be for some people, it does not remove the real struggles of others—of those hurting, crying hearts seeking honest answers! (And then, when answers come that are obviously right, they need to be accepted.)

Many of these questions will be discussed more specifically in later chapters. For now, here are some general thoughts.

Practical Observations

In spite of the questions we face at times, a little thought will probably assure us that God understands our emotions better than we do. Things are not necessarily as bad as they feel. God is eager to help us in our needy areas. The Bible says, "Like as a father pitieth his children, so the LORD pitieth them that fear him. For he knoweth our frame; he remembereth that we are dust" (Psalm 103:13, 14). That is the good news.

Let's go back to Elijah. How did God deal with him? He could have rebuked Elijah for his narrow, selfish thinking. Or He could have given him what he asked for—death. But He didn't. When Elijah lay down to sleep in utter discouragement, God sent an angel to wake Elijah and feed him, not once, but twice. He led Elijah gently and brought him back to usefulness. Does that give us any hope? It should.

Or look at Jonah. Jonah actually got angry and said some very harsh things to God when He did not destroy Nineveh as Jonah had predicted. Rather than punishing Jonah, God graciously made a gourd grow up to shadow him as he sat pouting on the hillside. God wanted Jonah to understand that He was treating the people of Nineveh the same way Jonah wanted to be treated.

Still, the question lingers: Does our emotional condition become a salvation issue and endanger our relationship with the Lord? This question needs to be answered cautiously because we do not want to stifle the grace of God, underestimating what He can or will do. God is very gracious with people, as we saw in the case of Elijah and Jonah. But neither do we want to stretch the grace of God to cover sin.

The answer lies not so much in the emotions themselves but in what our emotions influence us to do. For example, to say, “Sorry, my emotions ran away with me” does not excuse immorality. To say, “I couldn’t help it” does not excuse losing one’s temper. If we follow misguiding emotions into sin and refuse to repent, we are endangering our salvation.

By now we might think our emotions cause us more problems than they do us good! However, we can’t get rid of them, as we could get rid of an ailing arm or leg. Emotions are an integral part of us. And really, if we stop and think it through, would we want to get rid of them? Probably not!

We want to be sure our emotions do not lead us in the wrong direction, for they have the power to do that if not remedied. And we want to look for the practical answers to these struggles so that we can enjoy the blessings of being free indeed!

Chapter
Eight

Freedom and the Blues

Monday was usually a bad day for Elaine. She felt like a miserable failure. Things looked dark and foreboding. Nothing seemed worth doing, and she had to push herself to keep going. The children seemed extra edgy and demanding. Her patience wore thin. By evening she was exhausted.

Did Sunday have something to do with it? Sunday was usually an active day with worship services and related activities. She was an inspiration to others and thoroughly enjoyed it all. But Monday . . .

Andrew was a stable, active man quietly raising his family on their own small acreage close to the church. He was appreciated and used in a variety of ways. He fit well into a local contractor's business and carried a fair bit of responsibility.

But occasionally Andrew felt like a flat tire. He couldn't get excited about anything. Going to work was a chore, and giving himself to his family when he came home was difficult. His wife tried to involve him, but he had a hard time seeing a purpose in life.

He couldn't explain it. He really didn't have that much to complain about; and since he wasn't a complainer, he suffered in silence. He tried to be pleasant and sociable. Many around him would have been surprised if they had known how he felt inside.

Did he like himself for it? Of course not. But he couldn't seem to shake it.

The blues are not confined to mothers and fathers. Young, old, married, and single people all face them. They don't necessarily come at predictable times, but can come at unexpected and inopportune times. Possibly no one is immune to them.

How Do the Blues Affect Freedom?

Is it wrong to feel blue? It certainly feels wrong to be robbed of our joy!

At such times, it is quite easy to look around and see how good others have it. They don't seem to be plagued with our problems. They always seem to be on top of things, and nothing gets them down. The psalmist said in Psalm 73, "But as for me, my feet were almost gone; my steps had well nigh slipped. For I was envious at the foolish, when I saw the prosperity of the wicked."

There may be days when we, like the psalmist, find little to be glad about and much to complain about. We become shortsighted. The clouds block out the sun and the bright sky beyond. Life becomes distorted, and our troubles crowd to the forefront of our minds. At such times, our troubles, whether real or imagined, will keep our souls in prison if we let them.

Are the blues the result of spiritual problems? Should our spiritual nature be the overriding power so that our emotions are always under its control? Does anything less than this point to spiritual problems?

It is true that spiritual problems can be the source of emotional difficulties. But we must be cautious about making such an assumption. Let's face a few facts.

Our emotions can be affected by weariness. Soul, body, and spirit all affect each other. When our bodies and minds get tired, our emotions feel it. So we don't need to get excited about it if we can no longer get excited! At those times, we can look forward to feeling better again.

By the way, it has been observed that a certain amount of depression can be good for you because it slows you down and gives you a rest. (Some people don't take to that suggestion very well.) One man likened emotional tempo to the seasons of the year. He said there is a time of renewal in the spring, growth and harvest in the summer and fall, and then rest in the winter.

Our emotions are progress-oriented. We like to see results. If we work all day with few results, we feel low. One writer submitted a lengthy work to a publisher, only to have them reject it. The writer was so discouraged that he burned the manuscript. We all react like that sometimes to lack of progress. (Note: Later the publishers changed their minds and wanted the manuscript!)

One time we were building a concrete wall. We spent considerable time putting forms into place before pouring the concrete. Finally, when we were pouring the last of the concrete, the form broke and the concrete gushed out the bottom. Our emotions slid down with the concrete! All that work for nothing—except we had to quickly get the concrete out of the way before it hardened, so we could start again.

Our emotions are sensitive. Some people get blue over a psychological scratch. Someone rebukes or humiliates them. Their skin is too thin, and their feelings are too close to the surface to handle it. Most of us can remember times when we responded like that too. With growth in the grace of God, our ability increases to not take everything personally or too seriously.

The blues may result from an unexplainable sag in our spirits. In Psalm 142:3, the psalmist said, "When my spirit was overwhelmed within me, then thou knewest my path." Was he guilty of something? Was the situation as bad as it seemed? We don't know, but the context leaves us thinking that the problem was primarily his feelings, not some burden of guilt.

The blues may come from an avalanche of feelings. Our emotions can be like the concrete forms or a dam that holds so much and then bursts—and the outburst can stir up a lot of silt and dirt. Something can come along that triggers old memories or old pains and, to our disappointment, stirs a burst of feelings in our mind.

Times like these, whether they involve a mild case of the blues or deep grief, can put motivation out of gear. Nothing seems to be worth doing anymore. A well-known writer once remarked that no one had warned him about the laziness of grief.

The blues may result from an eclipse of faith. Matters that are manageable when we see them through the eyes of faith can quickly appear unmanageable when we lose our God's-eye view of the situation. When our faith sags, our emotions will too.

Emotions can become overloaded. Electric motors have overload switches. When the requirements are greater than their abilities, they shut down. Whether we like it or not, our emotions have limitations. Constant tension, crisis situations, and prolonged difficulties bring stress. Some people handle such pressures better than others, but even they are affected by them. If we do not find ways to deal with the pressures of life, our emotions will be affected. Although they might not shut down like a switch, there comes a time to pay attention to the load they are carrying.

Those who do not respect their limitations and find practical answers for the stresses in their lives end up with their emotions spiraling out of control. We don't want to be such victims if we can help it. That is why we need to look for answers about being bogged down by the blues.

Coping With the Blues

Since the threat of the blues is personal for each individual, there are no simple, one-size-fits-all answers. However, here are some suggestions that can help you avoid or deal with the blues.

Don't panic if you feel blue. The feeling may pass as quickly and quietly as it came. Go on with life, and don't spend your time waiting for it to get worse. Don't bother trying to tabulate your emotional pulse. Go on and live.

It has been observed that some people feel bluest as the day begins to wane. Probably you yourself can remember certain late afternoons in gray, slushy February, when your spirits felt low. Once night fell and the lights came on, you felt a little better. The point—wait patiently for it to get better.

Recognize the symptoms. Watch for the signals that precede the blues. Pay attention to what brings them on. Then work at stopping the starts. It is like one man who had a drinking problem. One of his downward steps was that he always started smoking again before he went back to drinking. By dealing with the smoking problem, he avoided the other. Others who have had severe problems found that after learning what the signals were, they were able to avoid the real thing.

In our early years in the Northwest, we would find ourselves in an emotional vacuum after visitors left. While they were with us, everything bustled. But when they left, everything seemed quiet, and we wandered around, hardly knowing where to pick up. We found that planning an extra-busy day when company left helped us immensely.

Hold court with your feelings. Don't just take their word. Force yourself to test whether your feelings are telling the truth. If they are exaggerating, admit it and deal with them. If you don't, they will drag you deeper.

Do something worthwhile. Force yourself to do something constructive. It may be cleaning up the sink or the desk or the shop. (Needing to clean up may have caused some of your gloomy feelings in the first place.)

Be thankful. Matthew Henry was once mugged and robbed, but he was thankful. He said he was glad the robbers didn't take much, because he didn't have much. He was glad, too, that he was still alive, and that he was the robbed one and not the robber. "Count your blessings" is not just old advice; it is good medicine.

Do something for someone else. The blues often result from thinking too much about oneself. Help someone who needs help. Maybe it will help you see you don't have all the trouble.

Incidentally, you won't help him or yourself if you pour all your woes on him. Recently I visited a friend in the hospital. He was feeling a little blue because no answers for his problem had surfaced. While I was there, an older man also dropped in and spent at least fifteen minutes telling my sick friend all he had been through. (I was surprised he survived it all!) He likely thought it would comfort the sick patient to hear that someone had had it worse than he. But when the well-meaning man left, my friend rolled his eyes!

Take your burden to the Lord. He is just as eager to relieve you of small anxieties and distresses as He is to relieve you of big ones. Go to Him as a friend. Seek Him in

Bible reading and prayer. Remember that the Bible says, in Hebrews 4:15, that Jesus went through it all and "was in all points tempted like as we are, yet without sin."

Claim the promises of God. They are sure because God gave them. Take inventory of God's faithfulness to His promises in the past. Join the psalmist (Psalm 121:1, 2): "I will lift up mine eyes unto the hills, from whence cometh my help. My help cometh from the LORD, which made heaven and earth."

Put a motto on your wall, or at least on the wall of your mind, that says, "The future is as bright as the promises of God!"

Believe the promises! Live in them. Live for them and by them. There is power in them—power to make us free indeed!

Chapter Nine

Freedom and Trouble

"Have mercy upon me, O Lord, for I am in trouble: mine eye is consumed with grief, yea, my soul and my belly" (Psalm 31:9).

The psalmist David knew what his trouble was. He talked to himself about it in terms like these: "Why art thou cast down, O my soul? and why art thou disquieted in me?" (Psalm 42:5). Apparently though, he could not easily talk himself out of his troubles, for in the following verse he confessed, "O my God, my soul *is* cast down within me." He realized he needed more than self-talk. He turned to the Lord for help.

When trouble takes over in our lives, we are in trouble! It takes control of our minds and hearts and spoils our freedom in the Lord. But there is hope!

David found his way through his troubles. God has ways for us too.

> When trouble takes over in our lives, we are in trouble!

It is our tendency when we have trouble to ask, "Why me?" or "What did I do wrong that this happened to me?" There is an honest way to ask these questions, but if we are just whining and pitying ourselves, we will not make our troubles go away by focusing on them.

Face it: troubles are a fact of life. This sounds too elementary to mention—until you discover that some people don't quite believe it. They seem to figure that if they do everything just right and are fortunate, they will slip through life with very few troubles. One father had to tell his daughter, "If you faced the fact that life is hard, things would be much easier for you."

Job said it right: "What? shall we receive good at the hand of God, and shall we not receive evil?" (Job 2:10). If Job had not understood this, he would not have survived his troubles. He would have blamed God and hated Him for his troubles.

Jacob understood the same thing. He told Pharaoh, in Genesis 47:9, "The days of the years of my pilgrimage are an hundred and thirty years: few and evil have the days of the years of my life been, and have not attained unto the days of the years of the life of my fathers in the days of their pilgrimage."

God has not given His children immunity from the painful experiences in life. They too have the normal troubles of humanity—accidents, tragedies, poverty, sickness, aging, and death. They have difficulties and disappointments along with everybody else.

Trouble is not proof that there is something wrong with us and that God is punishing us for it. While godly living delivers us from many troubles, we are still vulnerable to them. And likely, if we had all the troubles we deserved, things would be a lot worse!

If you think you have no troubles, perhaps everything has been going your way recently. Be glad while it lasts, because it probably will not stay that way. Then too, perhaps you have learned to reduce your troubles by facing them realistically and not being devastated by them. Be glad about that, and be ready to help others with their troubles!

Why Trouble Affects Our Freedom

Even if we admit that trouble is a fact of life, we can be taken aback when trouble comes. What makes it so hard to accept the particular troubles we have?

It is easier to talk about trouble than to handle it when it comes. But even the thought of trouble strikes raw nerves within. The insurance world thrives on it. Try to go to sleep after listening to an insurance salesman describe the need for a house-fire warning system. Even the thought of trouble can displace the freedom in our minds.

Trouble interferes with our lives. It interrupts and inconveniences us. When do we have time to get sick or have flat tires? We project doing pleasant things that make us productive. Trouble threatens our freedom by delaying us in the things we were planning to do. It threatens the resources we have plans for.

Trouble gets our attention because it hurts. It may affect our bodies, our schedules, our pocketbooks, or someone we care about. It begs for a response, for relief, and for a remedy.

Troubles remind us that we are not in control— that we can't cope with or escape from some things. Bad health, for example, hurts because it reminds us that we are not in total control of our bodies. Old people in particular are confronted with this lesson. Job spoke of this aspect of life when he said in the midst of his troubles, "God maketh my heart soft" (Job 23:16). God used him to show us how hard it can be when things don't go well.

Troubles threaten the good and pleasant things in our lives. We enjoy the security of our surroundings, our families, and the many things we are apt to take for granted. If it were not for trouble, our lives would be much more secure.

Troubles seem wrong, somehow. And they *are* wrong because they are the result of sin. The Bible tells us, in John 11:35, that Jesus wept with those who were weeping for Lazarus. Were His tears more than mere grief? Were His tears the result of seeing in Lazarus's death the tragedy of the power of death? Whatever the case, Jesus raised him up (as He did many others) in a demonstration of His power over death. In the final analysis, God sees death as an enemy, as all other troubles are.

Troubles are all too real. A strong creek that runs through our property was suddenly blocked by a fallen tree. The stream soon found its way around the fallen tree by cutting a new channel, doing much damage to the surrounding land. Sometimes, when trouble pushes people into a tight spot, they—like our creek—take a course they never intended to take. Instead of trouble making them better, it makes them worse. And to add to that, the way back to the previous course can be hard.

Since troubles take us by surprise, they tend to multiply their proportions. They can look bigger than they are and can make us feel as if we have the worst troubles in the world. They can keep us from seeing that we have more good things than trouble.

Before we discuss staying spiritually and emotionally free in trouble, we must consider a haunting question that is often raised: "Where is God when there is trouble?" Sadly, this question has taken some people further away from the very thing they wanted.

Is God in Our Troubles?

Did God create trouble? Does He like to agitate and frustrate us?

In the beginning, the way God created things, there was no trouble. Everything was perfect! So the answer to our questions is clear: God is not the cause of trouble. Trouble was the result of human actions. That is the way it still is today. Even though trouble began as a result of the Fall in the Garden of Eden, we have a way of bringing a fair amount of trouble on ourselves.

God has put laws of cause and effect into place. If we go barefoot in the snow, we should not be surprised if we catch a cold. If we neglect replacing worn-out tires, we might have an accident that could have been avoided. If we ignore safety measures in our homes, our children may be injured unnecessarily. It would be foolish for us to blame God for the repercussions of our neglect.

No, God does not cause our troubles. But He does allow troubles to come—even troubles that are not our fault—for reasons that we may never understand entirely. Although we will suggest a few reasons later in the chapter, let us rest assured that God has reasons above and beyond our imagination.

Of course Satan has his reasons too. It was Satan who introduced trouble, and he is a master at using trouble to turn people against God. Yet God is the only one who can really help us in our trouble! How quickly people think about blaming God for their troubles, yet it never seems to occur to them to think of God and give Him the credit for their good things!

Is God in our troubles? In one sense, yes—He is in them to help us! "God is our refuge and strength, a very present help in trouble" (Psalm 46:1). God can help us to have freedom in our hearts while we have trouble—even if we caused it. That is, if we look for it at the right place in the right way.

Finding Freedom in Trouble

Freedom begins with the way we view a situation. We can say, as Jacob once did, "All these things are against me," or we can see further than that. Stumbling blocks can sometimes be made into steppingstones. Even though it is painful and we may be slow to recognize it, we will be better and stronger after we master our troubles than we were before.

What things should we do to find the freedom God wants us to have in our troubles? That is, not only after the trouble, but while we are in it!

Trust the promises of God. Here are just a few of them.

"Be strong and of a good courage, fear not, nor be afraid of them: for the LORD thy God, he it is that doth go with thee; he will not fail thee, nor forsake thee" (Deuteronomy 31:6).

"But my God shall supply all your need according to his riches in glory by Christ Jesus" (Philippians 4:19).

"And we know that all things work together for good to them that love God, to them who are the called according to his purpose" (Romans 8:28).

This last, oft-quoted promise still holds good. We believe that God can make good come out of every situation in His own way and in His own time.

Some people tell us we do not know how hard life can be. That is true. We don't. But the Lord does. "In all their affliction he was afflicted, and the angel of his presence saved them" (Isaiah 63:9).

Accept what God has allowed to happen. Loretta is a middle-aged woman we met while holding a service at a care center for aged and infirm persons. She is the mother of six children. But she was stricken with muscular dystrophy and is confined to total care. She sits stiffly in her chair with her head tilted backward. She can barely move her hand. She cannot eat and must be fed through a tube. She has little hope of getting better.

But she smiles as she talks in a whisper! How does she cope with her trouble? She expresses faith in God and, through her tears and smiles, says, "Whatever!" That is her anchor, her word of acceptance to God. Can you understand why we went away feeling ministered to more than we had ministered?

Believe that God is at work. When Joseph was sold to the Midianites by his brothers, he could have spent the rest of his life in self-pity and bitterness. But what he told his brothers years later reveals the secret of his strength. Regardless of how long it had taken him to realize it, he saw God's hand in it all. He said to his brothers, in Genesis 50:20, "But as for you, ye thought evil against me: but God meant it unto good, to bring to pass, as it is this day, to save much people alive."

Forgive those who created the trouble. Joseph forgave his brothers. Jesus forgave His executioners. His disciples, ever since, have done the same. Without forgiveness, we can never get out of the cruel prison of resentment and hatred.

Recently a local father was traveling with his five children to a nearby city to meet his wife. An oncoming truck crossed the median strip and hit them, killing all five children almost instantly. In the eyes of the community, the driver should have been punished severely. But would the parents find freedom in seeing him prosecuted to the limit? Their only true freedom lay in forgiving the driver. Otherwise, their hearts would have been haunted with bitterness and hatred. By God's grace, they chose His way of forgiveness.

Let God use your trouble to attract the world's attention. When God's children relate properly to trouble, the world notices. Along the highway where the five children died in the crash, five crosses now stand, accompanied by a sign that says, "Forgiveness to all." People shake their heads and readily admit that only God could help parents to accept the loss that way. The love and composure of believers facing a crisis has often caused others to marvel at God's grace.

Let God use your trouble to redirect your course. In Psalm 119:67, David admitted he needed this redirection: "Before I was afflicted I went astray: but now have I kept thy word." We may not know all God is doing in our lives, but sometimes He causes our hopes and dreams to crumble at His feet because He has a better way. He may be steering us closer to Himself and away from something that endangers us.

The apostle Paul wanted to visit Rome. No doubt he had ideas about how to get there. Did he expect to go there in chains? Hardly, but God brought him to Rome as a prisoner. Nevertheless, Paul's spirit was not bound. He kept ministering to persons at the end of his chain—soldiers, fellow prisoners, visitors—and thereby reached many people. Had he looked at his situation negatively, he would not have been any good to anyone. Instead, the prison became his pulpit for God.

From Rome, Paul wrote how he looked at his trouble: "But I would ye should understand, brethren, that the things which happened unto me have fallen out rather unto the furtherance of the gospel; so that my bonds in Christ are manifest in all the palace, and in all other places" (Philippians 1:12, 13). He went on to explain how God was working through it all—and that he was the willing participant!

The Philippians should have understood this well, because about ten years before, God had used a prison in their city to bring a jailer and his household to Himself. In the inner prison, with their feet in stocks, Paul and Silas prayed and sang, and at midnight God moved. (See Acts 16.) What if they had been crushed by their trouble?

Look for what God may be trying to teach you. Why do things not go well? Perhaps God is telling us we are trying to do too much. We may need to lower or realign our goals. On the other hand, perhaps God is teaching us patience and wants our simple cooperation. Perhaps God is teaching us to be more careful in our daily, practical responsibilities.

See trouble as an opportunity to grow. So something does not work? Look for a better solution. See failure, not as a locked door, but as an open door. What kept Thomas Edison going back to his laboratory day and night while working on the light bulb? He said that each failure taught him something that did not work! Seeing life that way gives enthusiasm and freedom.

Take your share of the blame for trouble. When there is trouble, we are apt to look for someone to blame—preferably someone else. Next time, instead of saying, "You should have checked the fuel gauge," try saying, "I should have checked the fuel gauge." There is real freedom in accepting our share of responsibility.

In summary, if we believe that God is in our troubles for our good and His glory, we can have peace and freedom in the midst of difficulty. Since we do not know what form trouble will come in, we must be walking with the Lord constantly through cloud and sunshine. Our relationship with Him must be kept current by faith, repentance, and obedience to Him. Then we can trust Him to be there for all our needs.

It is the only way to truly be free!

CHAPTER TEN

Freedom and the Fear of Making Mistakes

No one likes to fail. We avoid it when we can. The sheer fear of failure can paralyze and cripple our growth and usefulness. It can keep us from having the freedom that God wants us to have.

This chapter is about the fear of making mistakes. It is about our fear of not measuring up to our own expectations and what we perceive to be the expectations of others. It is not about the fear of sinning, although the sin of pride may be lurking under our fear of failure. It is about living in freedom even if we are not perfect by social and industry standards.

The fear of failure is not a new problem. When God directed Moses to tell Pharaoh to let Israel go, Moses had a list of excuses. Most of them were prompted by the fear of failure. God had to become downright stern with him before he consented to go. Jeremiah had a similar problem. "Ah, Lord God!" he said, "I cannot speak: for I am a child" (Jeremiah 1:6). Both men had to get past their fears in order to function.

We need to do the same. Franklin was a sincere young man with high aspirations to serve the Lord. But he was afraid to try anything new. He would have liked to try song leading; but even when he was asked to do it, he hedged. He had watched others do it and often felt he could lead singing as well as some of them. But when he thought of getting up and doing it, he was afraid it would be a flop.

Franklin could not bear the thought of not doing it just right. He feared that even if people did not laugh at him outright, they might laugh behind his back. He still carried keen memories from his school days when he had been laughed at for his clumsiness on the playground. He had determined then that he would avoid such situations at all costs.

This fear followed him. On the job, he was very reluctant to run a new piece of machinery. He would have liked to try it, but he feared he would fail. He envied others for the way they would rush into new opportunities with no more experience than he. But when his employer offered him the opportunity, he chose to stay with what he knew.

In social life, he also felt handicapped. He found it hard to say anything in a crowd of people. It wasn't that he didn't know anything—it was getting it said! He feared that someone would counter or criticize what he said. So it was easier to keep quiet. It was well-nigh impossible for him to share his deepest feelings.

Franklin was attracted to a sincere, respectable woman who was a member of his home congregation. But again he was afraid. The fear that she might not share his interest and might turn him down sent him into a whirl and kept him from sharing his interest with her.

The fear of failure stifled Franklin. He knew he was not growing as he should. He felt trapped. Why was it like this?

How Does Fear of Failure Take Away Freedom?

Fear of failure hinders our freedom to be ourselves. When we fear, we tend to lock up. People who speak in public sometimes say that when they get up to speak, their thinker sits down! Fear that we might not do something just right takes away our freedom to respond to situations spontaneously. So we become afraid to try. And the longer we hesitate, the worse it gets! For instance, we know we should talk to a stranger at church, but what if we blush or stammer? Perhaps the best prayer to pray at such a time is "Help, Lord; here goes."

Fear of failure can hinder our freedom to grow. It can keep us from trying to do something we have not done before. It may keep us from reaching the potential God has in mind for us. He wants to lead us into broader fields of growth and opportunity, just as we want to lead our own children into greater achievements. He will be disappointed if we, His sons and daughters, are never ready to let Him stretch us. That is why the parent eagles push their eaglets out of the nest. It is the only way to learn to fly.

Fear of failure takes away our freedom to relax. When we don't relax, we do even worse than usual. We become stilted, artificial, and clumsy. Whether in public or private, we function better when we don't feel pressured about failing. If the fear of failure rules us, we become so self-conscious that it makes it hard to do what we are trying to do. It reminds me of a time my brother climbed the huge maple tree by our house. He shinnied up to the top, where the trunk swayed in the breeze. But when he got there and looked down, he froze. Suddenly he was afraid! He couldn't bear to look down to see where to put his foot for the next lower step. He clung there until his older brother coaxed and coached him for each step back down to his comfort zone.

You may be thinking, "But really, a certain amount of fear is good. It can be dangerous to feel too free high in the air and become careless." That's right. Some people have the same problem behind the wheel of a vehicle. They feel like they are in total control—and then drive as if nothing can go wrong. And when some people feel too free with their tongues, they say more than they ought!

That's the "over-confident" ditch on the other side of the road. So really, it might be safer on the "fear" side. But we believe that God has a comfortable place for us between the two extremes which enables us to be our best for Him. That is the freedom we are thinking about here.

Why Do We Fear Failure?

That's a good question. Do we fear it because no one else around us makes mistakes? Hardly. Do we fear it because others think we are perfect and we would disappoint them if we failed? Probably not. Do we fear it because of how we look at others when they fail? Hopefully not.

Do we fear failure because we think it would damage our image? Are we afraid of what others might think if we failed? Think slowly before answering, "What image?" Sometimes it's hard to recognize our sensitivity to keeping a good image.

Do we fear failure because we have projected ourselves to be more than we really are? Have we been acting as if we knew a good bit about something? Have we criticized others who were doing it? Now suddenly it is our turn to try. But it might not hurt us to fail!

We might fear failure lest we fall short of our own high standards—and the high standards we think others have for us. For example, in my earlier days, I operated numerous types of equipment. Recently someone gave me the opportunity to run a newer machine than I was used to. I was reluctant to try, because I was afraid it wouldn't go well. I didn't know if the "touch" was still there. So it would have been easy to refuse, to save embarrassment. Either way doesn't hurt us. We can decline or try. It does not hurt us to acknowledge that we are no longer capable of doing certain things.

In the opening paragraphs, we hinted that sin could lie beneath our fear of failure. It could be pride. We need to be suspicious of ourselves.

Of course, one might honestly underestimate his abilities. A Sunday school superintendent asked an older man to teach a Sunday school class. He declined because he was sure he could not do it. The superintendent asked him if he had ever felt he could do as well as others when they were teaching. He said that no, he never had! So he did not try.

But sometimes it is good to stretch our abilities. Several other people in that congregation did try, even though they became very lightheaded in front of an audience. (Their discomfort was so obvious that it made us nervous for fear they might faint!) But they tried again and again, and now they can do what fear told them they could not do.

Coping With the Fear of Failure

To overcome fear, we must overcome what we fear. If we fear the dark, we must face the dark frankly, ignoring what fear whispers to us about the dark. One wise man introduced a child to the interesting night sounds and turned the fearful darkness into a friendly, adventuresome place.

If we fear failing, we need to consider what is so bad about failing. Has anyone ever really learned to do anything without failing at times? No. Learning and progress are always made on the shoulders of trial and error. Someone said, “The reason some people haven’t succeeded is because they haven’t failed often enough.”

Always be determined to try again. One of my childhood memories is being taught, “If at first you don’t succeed, try, try again.” What if we had quit trying to tie our shoes when we failed the first time someone showed us?

The wise man said it better yet, in Proverbs 24:16: “For a just man falleth seven times, and riseth up again.” Rises again! There is the key. Anyone can (and does) go down in failure. It is those who get up again that make it.

See failure as a step to success. No one enjoys failing, but we should see it as a necessary part of the process. A mother expects some broken dishes when her child is learning to help. A father should be prepared to accept some damage while his son is learning. My father seemed to make instinctive judgments as to whether our mistakes were carelessness or lack of foresight. His response was affected by how much he felt we cared.

God expects adults to make mistakes too. His question is not so much, “How much damage have you done?” as “How much have you learned from this experience?”

Believe that accepting failure is a mark of maturity. How do we look at someone who fails and is humble about it? Do we disdain him? Or do we admire him for facing up to it? Why then is it so hard to admit our own failure?

Seek God’s approval. Accepting failure has much to do with whose approval we seek. If we want people to always think well of us, we will have problems accepting failure lest it put us in a bad light. But if we seek God’s approval first of all and most of all, we need not worry about what others might think of us. Even when we are misunderstood or feel misrepresented, God knows. How liberating it is to put it all into His hands!

Forget about image polishing. This takes us back to the "What image?" question. We need to seek deliverance from trying to impress others. If we are beyond that, personal failure will not take us down very far, because we were never very high in the first place. If we learn not to take ourselves too seriously, our step will be much lighter. John Bunyan told how he was delivered from both praises and criticism. "If my life is fruitless, it doesn't matter who praises me; and if my life is fruitful, it doesn't matter who criticizes me."

Give life your best. When we are confident that God knows we are doing our best, we need not be afraid of failure or imperfection. God is like a parent who gets a smudged drawing or a bouquet of weeds from a loving child: He knows the spirit behind it! Neither do we need to fear to try something new. We need not fear stumbling, because we know He is there to help us get going again.

When we surrender all to God—even our failures—we can have freedom. When we sincerely care about pleasing Him, we are in the presence of a great Rock that overshadows all the other things we might fear. Then, what else matters?

That is being free indeed!

Chapter Eleven

Freedom From Hurts of the Past

"If the Son therefore shall make you free, ye shall be free indeed" (John 8:36).

Nobody can completely escape from his past. Why should we want to? Even if we had absolutely no pleasant memories, we would still need information from the past to help us understand today. Without a past, you would not know how to read this book, nor would you know how to relate the advice in this book to anything you know, for you would know nothing.

Even though our past is valuable to us, unpleasant things from our past can haunt us. The more we try to forget them, the more they might trouble us. That is where the emotions can get involved. Of course, if we have done wrong that has not been resolved, we have to deal with guilt. But sometimes we have to deal with wrongs done to us. These can tempt us to emotions of bitterness, resentment, and hatred. They may erode the feeling of self-confidence and turn it into despair.

Satan does his best to use whatever part of our past he can to bring us into emotional bondage. And we all have things to deal with in our past, even if we think we had an ideal past.

Let me explain. A person with the best kind of past may have to deal with pride. He may think that because of his past, he is somehow better than others. The apostle Paul had that problem for years. But after his conversion, this changed. When he gave his credentials in Philippians 3, he listed things some people would have thought made him impeccably good. But he concluded that they did him no good and had to be discarded.

Prior to his conversion, he had trusted in his background for his credibility and acceptance by God. He thought it authorized him to kill those who did not agree with him. His good opinion of himself during those years caused him much grief later.

Paul had another problem after his conversion—remorse for the realization of how wicked he had been in the past. He could have allowed that to haunt him into uselessness. But he didn't! He made peace with God and served Him powerfully.

Remorse for the Past

Everybody has to deal with remorse, because we have all done wrong. Romans 3:23 settles that. "For all have sinned, and come short of the glory of God." Even though we know the past cannot be changed, the deep sorrow and regret for the past stays with us. There is a constructive side and a destructive side to this.

Some people suffer bitter remorse for wasted years—years that could have been spent laying a foundation for the future. Along with that comes remorse for what those years were filled with—sin, selfishness, serving the flesh. The seeds that were sown then may now be producing a harvest of physical problems, broken homes, and tarnished reputations, all adding to their remorse.

The good news is that there is a remedy for remorse—the blessed privilege of forgiveness for the past through the blood of Jesus. Even though the regret continues, the sting of guilt is removed.

Regret for the past is good because it helps us to shun sin and do right. It stimulates us to praise the Lord for His forgiveness and to follow Him faithfully.

Memories After Being Forgiven

Normally, memory is a wonderful thing. But memory can haunt the mind. Even after people come to Christ and receive forgiveness for their sins, the memories of past misdeeds may still linger. Memories can be cruel if they are not dealt with properly.

In fact, memories can be so strong that they refresh the feelings of guilt and make it hard to believe that the old sins are forgiven. They may stir doubt in the heart about one's relationship with the Lord. The past becomes a haunting cloud over the soul. And that cloud must be dispelled if we are to have joy.

The apostle Paul spoke of his past at times. He expressed deep regret over the way he had persecuted Christians. His memories could have discouraged him. Maybe that is why, in Philippians 3:13, he said, "Brethren, I count not myself to have apprehended: but this one thing I do, forgetting those things which are behind, and reaching forth unto those things which are before . . ."

He acknowledged his past, but he looked back on it through the eyes of faith. He trusted that he was forgiven.

He said, in 1 Corinthians 15:9, "For I am the least of the apostles, that am not meet [worthy] to be called an apostle, because I persecuted the church of God." He solved the problem in the very next verse: "But by the grace of God I am what I am!" There is no better answer to the failures of the past than the present grace of God.

Paul put it even more plainly in 1 Timothy 1:13–15: "Who [I, Paul] was before a blasphemer, and a persecutor, and injurious. . . . And the grace of our Lord was exceeding abundant with faith and love which is in Christ Jesus. This is a faithful saying, and worthy of all acceptation, that Christ Jesus came into the world to save sinners."

Past deeds that have been forgiven and washed away by the blood of Jesus need to be left with Him!

Sometimes it is not the guilt, but the allurements of the past, that catch our attention. Satan and the flesh try to drag us back once more to revel in the memory of secret, fleshly pleasures. We may be tempted to slyly boast of things or glory in things we ought to be ashamed of. Of course, such actions stir emotions of guilt. This kind of problem can only find answers at the foot of the cross in constant, ongoing repentance. We must treat our memories the same way Paul treated his.

Memories of past failures can be a blessing if they help us to be broken before God. They remind us of our past and present weaknesses. Understanding this draws us to God for strength.

Hurts From the Past

Everyone has been hurt or wronged in the past. We may have been cheated, lied to, lied about, made fun of, or treated unfairly in some other way. It is surprising how much these things can hurt. Yet these are nothing compared to the problems some people have faced.

Many people have been grossly violated in immoral ways in the past. They were abused and victimized in shameful ways, often by someone they trusted. The perpetrator may have gone his way and left the victim with painful, haunting memories. With the memories may come shame and a burdensome, crippling sense of worthlessness. It is common for such victims to blame themselves for what happened, even though most times they were totally innocent. If it is an abiding problem, further help should be sought.

What if the victim willingly cooperated in the abuse? In such cases, even though the perpetrator is primarily to blame, it is right for the victim to take whatever part of the blame is his. Repentance toward God and forgiveness toward the perpetrator are the keys for the victim to move beyond the pain.

Some cases of abuse would not have happened if someone who became aware of what was happening would have done something about it. The victim has to deal with the hurt toward that person as well; sometimes that may be as hard as dealing with the perpetrator.

Somehow this part of one's past must be disposed of properly. Even if the guilty party does not come forward in repentance, answers need to be found. That answer is not found in hatred nor in justice; it can only come by forgiveness!

Forgiveness for who? First of all, to have freedom, we all must have forgiveness from God—whoever we are and for whatever we have done. After that, we must consider the past forgiven and go on with life. Sometimes that may be the hardest part.

Beyond that, who else must forgive who? Hard as it might seem, we know the answer to that. The wronged person must forgive the person who did him wrong. Jesus told us we must forgive if we want to be forgiven. "For if ye forgive men their trespasses, your heavenly Father will also forgive you: but if ye forgive not men their trespasses, neither will your Father forgive your trespasses" (Matthew 6:14, 15). He also showed us how it is done when He prayed for those who were crucifying Him: "Father, forgive them."

Forgiveness does not overlook a wrong with the words, "It doesn't matter." If indeed it doesn't matter, there's nothing to forgive. Neither is forgiveness merely a warm, fuzzy feeling toward a wrongdoer. Rather, forgiveness acknowledges the wrong done and then says, in effect, to the wrongdoer, "I won't make you pay. I set you free, between you and me. I wish only your good and pray that you will seek forgiveness from God so that you can enjoy a happy eternity."

Without doubt, this is much more easily said than done. Indeed, it can only be done by the love of God in the heart. Forgiveness is also probably not a once-and-done, forever-gone matter. A man who felt deeply wronged by another said to him, "I forgive you." Knowing the depth of the man's feelings, someone admonished him to say, "I am forgiving you," so that if negative feelings came up again, he would remember that he had committed himself to keep on forgiving.

In these situations, a trusted friend can help sort out feelings, steer thoughts in the right way, and then help to work it out. Forgiveness can be hard enough with a friend's help, let alone doing it by yourself.

Memories—Freedom After Forgiving

Memories seldom stay the same. Over a period of time, they fade. Like the paint on a house, they need to be refurbished to be kept. The real facts may become faint and a bit distorted. (At least that is what I've been told when I shared some of my long-ago memories!)

What am I getting at? We tend to remember what we prefer to remember, and ignore what we prefer to ignore. If we choose to focus on good memories, they become better with time. That makes the past a happy past and adds to our present happiness.

The opposite is also true. If we highlight the hurtful, disappointing things about our past, soon that will be all we can remember. Not only will our memories hurt more and more, they will also cast their shadow over our present lives.

We need to let go of the things that we cannot change, and focus on the good things that did happen during our growing-up years. Few people don't have at least a bit of good to cling to and build on—some special time with someone who cared. It may have been a family member, a grandparent, or a neighbor who gave us special attention—or helped us when we were in need. Look back, and bring that memory up to date!

Our ability to remember is like a garden. It can grow weeds without any attention. But plant the right seeds, keep the weeds out, water it well, and we have a beautiful, useful garden.

Look around you and find a happy person. Most likely, you will find that he has made peace with his past. Even if it was dark and difficult, he kept the good and disposed of the rest. And no doubt he is busy now making good memories for the future!

Again, if the past is too big for you to handle alone, seek help from someone who can lead you to the One who can truly help—the Lord Jesus Christ.

Then too, remember to live a life of freedom in Christ Jesus right now. Endeavor to live in such a way that does not create more regret. Do your best to stay current in your walk with the Lord. If you let the present pile up on you, the unwelcome past will gleefully jump on top of the pile.

We must walk and live in the Spirit. It is the only way to be truly free. That is why God tells us, "Finally, brethren, whatsoever things are true, whatsoever things are honest, whatsoever things are just, whatsoever things are pure, whatsoever things are lovely, whatsoever things are of good report; if there be any virtue, and if there be any praise, *think on these things*" (Philippians 4:8).

The next verse tells us what lies beyond the thinking. "Those things, which ye have both learned, and received, and heard, and seen in me, do: and the God of peace shall be with you." It is the *doing* that makes it all work!

Guaranteed, doing right helps to make pleasant memories—and will give you help in having freedom from the hurts of the past.

Chapter Twelve

Freedom and Spiritual Failure

"If we confess our sins, he is faithful and just to forgive us our sins, and to cleanse us from all unrighteousness" (1 John 1:9).

No, this chapter is not about freedom in spiritual failure; it is about finding freedom by dealing with failure so we can get on in life.

Satan works in the opposite way. First, he works hard to bring us to failure and then works harder yet to keep us there. Our emotions are a large part of that target.

When Joe saw Paul coming to work, something didn't seem right. The last few days had been that way too. Paul didn't have the usual gleam in his eye or the spring in his step. His shoulders sagged a bit. "Hmm." Joe decided to watch more closely because he really cared about Paul.

By break time, Joe was sure something was wrong. He noticed that Paul was unusually quiet and had a hard time concentrating on his work. He often stared out the window. He had to redo some of his work.

"Paul, would you drop by the office at noon?" Joe asked quietly.

Paul looked up, startled. "Why, yes, I guess."

At noon Joe said kindly, "Paul, you don't seem like yourself the last few days. Is something wrong?"

Paul's eyes dropped, and his shoulders drooped. Tears welled up in his eyes. "Yes, there is," Paul said hoarsely. "You know about the problem I have had with being honest.

And last week it happened again. I lied to my father. It's getting me down." Paul almost seemed relieved that it was out. "What shall I do? I can't take it anymore. I—I—" He sighed.

Do you know the feeling?

Failure Can Happen

Failure. Wrongdoing. Sin. The tendency is part of our nature. Even after conversion, the possibility of failure does not go away. "Wherefore let him that thinketh he standeth take heed lest he fall" (1 Corinthians 10:12). In fact, Satan seems to try all the harder to bring the believer down. And he capitalizes on whatever failures he sees in us to distress and discourage us.

Denying the possibility of failure does not solve the problem, because it amounts to denying the truth. "If we say that we have no sin, we deceive ourselves, and the truth is not in us" (1 John 1:8).

God was well aware of all this . Although He has made it possible that we do not need to sin, He has also made provision for those who stumble and fall. First John 2:1 reads, "My little children, these things write I unto you, that ye sin not. And if any man sin, we have an advocate with the Father, Jesus Christ the righteous." That provision is not about deliberate, planned, ongoing sin. It is for unplanned, painful failure that seeks cleansing.

The pain of sin goes deep. It weighs on our conscience and puts a heavy cloud over our lives. In this book, we are especially interested in how this weight affects our emotional freedom in the Lord. Mostly, of course, we want to think what can be done about it.

No doubt we understand that we should not push our emotions aside if we have not yet resolved our own guilt.

In that case, emotions are our friend. They produce an overall sick feeling similar to what an intense earache or toothache gives to the body. It begs for release. Psalm 32:3, 4 describes the feeling: "When I kept silence, my bones waxed old through my roaring all the day long. For day and night thy hand was heavy upon me: my moisture is turned into the drought of summer."

In the case of prolonged guilt, the emotions can become very unsettled. Since this is well known, some people are quick to conclude that sin is always the cause of emotional difficulty. Always? No. Often? Yes.

Dealing With Failure

First we must be ready to admit we have done wrong. This can be a problem because our carnal nature fights the fact tenaciously. Our old nature instinctively offers excuses, explanations, and exoneration for what we have done. Our old nature is like the 90 percent of the prisoners who will tell you they are innocent and should not be in prison!

"I did wrong." "I am guilty." "I sinned." These are among the hardest admissions to make unless we have a genuine regret and repentance for our actions. But repentance is the point we must come to.

And then we need to move on from there. We can claim the blood of Jesus for forgiveness and cleansing. "If we confess our sins, he is faithful and just to forgive us our sins, and to cleanse us from all unrighteousness" (1 John 1:9).

After receiving forgiveness by repenting and confessing to God, we may need to make restitution if we have wronged someone. The smallest restitutions can be the hardest to make because they seem too little to make a fuss about. Well, get advice if you do not know what to do, and put the thing behind you. The devil likes to ruin peace over a small item.

We may need to apologize for wrong attitudes or words. If we do, we should apologize frankly. Hedging tends to spoil the apology and leaves us wondering if we did it right. But after a full and frank apology, words cannot express the lifting of the weight and the lightness of heart that the freed can experience.

But sometimes our emotions are not in step with all this. They cannot keep up with all the transactions. Remember, emotions are feelings, no more. They are not always accurate, so we cannot trust them for the last word.

Sometimes our emotions balk at accepting guilt. One man, when confronted with the fact that he had lost his temper, responded, "Did I say that?" "Did I do that?"

But sometimes it works the other way around, and the conscience does not accept forgiveness. A young schoolgirl was confronted over a misdeed and then forgiven, but the teacher noticed that for some time afterward, the child still carried a white, scared look on her face. For adults too, after a matter has been cleared, the feelings may have a hard time accepting the fact. They still hang heavy over the heart. Sometimes for no good reason they ask, "Are you sure you did it right? Maybe you didn't deal with everything."

What can be done?

Needless to say, search the Scriptures for direction on how to deal with sin. Dig out the promises of the grace of God. Bathe in the love of God, revealed by sending Jesus to die for our sins. Believe that the blood of Jesus cleanses us. It may take more than one journey through the promises to finally satisfy our emotions.

It can be helpful to lay the whole thing out to a mature, trusted person and let that person judge the situation.

Often a calm, sensible friend can tell us a thing in a way that we cannot tell ourselves. Those we subject ourselves to in the body of believers ought to be giving us guidance in these matters.

We need to be careful, though, that we do not trust in our confession and restitution rather than in the blood of Jesus for forgiveness of sin. What we do is only the means of meeting God's conditions to have the blessed gift of forgiveness.

Some people have been shaken out of the problem of doubt when they realized that hedging about accepting the promise of forgiveness was actually making God a liar. Even in the throes of emotion, we would not want to be guilty of doubting God.

Of course, the best way to deal with the problem of failure is to do what we can to prevent it. God would rather keep us out of failure than help us out after we have crashed.

Avoiding Failure

There are things that can be done—that must be done—if we hope to avoid failure. Here are a few.

Analyze the steps that take you down. Recently we lost our way at a detour in the Seattle freeway system. We made several circuits to find our way out, and when we finally were out, we still did not know where we had gone wrong. It was frustrating. How could we avoid making the same mistake the next time? When it comes to spiritual failure, however, we are usually not so puzzled. If we are honest, we normally know that the trouble began when we listened to the wrong kind of music, or went to a wrong place, or spent too much time with the wrong people, or allowed a thought to linger too long.

Think how you could have avoided the fall. Were there any danger signals? Did your conscience warn you? And were you listening? What could you have done differently if you had thought ahead more?

Stay well-fed spiritually. That makes sin lose its appeal. When we are hungry, food is tantalizing. But when we are full, food loses its appeal. That is why it is better economically to do grocery shopping after a meal rather than before a meal; it prevents impulsive buying. I tried it recently, and it works! By the same token, keeping the spirit well-satisfied by living close to the Lord helps to keep our appetite for other things in check.

Claim the promises of God. Have victory verses on hand—in your mind and heart. Some people carry Bible verse cards to help them in this. Believe that God is more powerful than Satan. The Bible is true when it says, "Greater is he that is in you, than he that is in the world" (1 John 4:4).

Nurture a repulsion to wrong. We need to remind ourselves of the wickedness of sin rather than feeding on its allurements. Like Moses, we need to see that the pleasures of sin last but a short time, while their pain continues for a long time—potentially, even for eternity. We need to remember that sin is the highest priced "bargain" anyone will ever get, and that we will never find an enduring pleasure in sin. When sin knocks, answer it with these thoughts. That is what Jesus did. He said, "Get thee behind me, Satan: for it is written . . ." And then He quoted Scripture to him. And it worked!

Rejoice in the Lord. Thank Him constantly for forgiveness, cleansing, and new life. Once you have brought all your sins and needs to Him, enjoy the clear skies. After he had failed, David prayed, "Restore unto me the joy of thy salvation; and uphold me with thy free spirit." We may ask for the same thing.

Walk with the Lord. Every day, all day. We can find no better way to avoid failure. First John 1:7 tells what all it does for us: "But if we walk in the light, as he is in the light, we have fellowship one with another, and the blood of Jesus Christ his Son cleanseth us from all sin." Light, fellowship with other believers, and the precious blood of Jesus—all to set us free and keep us free!

"And ye shall know the truth, and the truth shall make you free. . . . If the Son therefore shall make you free, ye shall be free indeed."

CHAPTER THIRTEEN

Freedom in Disappointment

It is natural for us to dream and to scheme, to wish and to plan, and to envision and to expect. In fact, it is good. What motivation would life have without anticipation? That's why the Bible says, "Where there is no vision, the people perish" (Proverbs 29:18).

The problem is that life brings problems. That is why the title of this chapter is "Freedom *in* Disappointment" rather than "Freedom *From* or *Without* Disappointment"!

The disappointments we face often devastate our dreams and desires. If we do not come to terms with a disappointment, it can create serious emotional stress that competes with our peace and joy in the Lord. Depending on how we relate to such stress, it can take us captive and destroy our freedom. It can go like this:

Richard came home from work and sank into the nearest chair. He sighed deeply.

"What is wrong?" his wife asked. "Are you sick?"

Richard shook his head and looked up. "I told you the boss was going to lay one of us off because the new machine will eliminate one man." His wife nodded and waited for him to go on. "Well, today the boss told me I am out of a job in three days."

"Well, I thought you had job security!" his wife exclaimed. "Now what? How will we make our payments?" It was a gloomy household as they pondered their future. Even the little children felt the weight of the quietness.

Two days later, Richard burst in the door and almost knocked his little son off his feet. "What now?" his wife exclaimed.

"The boss changed his mind. He said I am to run the new machine!" You can imagine the change of mood in that house that night.

Richard's reactions were natural. All of us have feelings that react to being hired and fired. The question is, Must such circumstances completely rule our emotions, or can we find emotional freedom even when we are disappointed? Something tells us that simply riding the roller coaster is not what God intended. He wants His children, as the chapter title says, to have freedom *in* disappointment, not always freedom *from* it.

If we cannot find freedom in disappointment, what might happen to us?

Options of Disappointment

King Ahab wanted Naboth's vineyard. He made a good offer to Naboth, but Naboth turned it down. What did Ahab do when he got home? "He laid him down upon his bed, and turned away his face, and would eat no bread" (1 Kings 21:4).

His wife figured him out quickly. She asked, "Why is thy spirit so sad, that thou eatest no bread?"

Ahab's name has become synonymous with pouting. Friends of ours had boys who named one of their rabbits Ahab because if they offered him food he didn't want, he turned away and would not eat it!

King Ahab managed to get his vineyard anyway, but he never really got to enjoy it. Obviously, there are sobering results of responding wrongly to disappointment.

Disappointments can come from almost any direction. Here are some illustrations.

We were looking forward to visiting with relatives from a distance, and then they called and said they were too sick to come. It was an adjustment after all the energy and anticipation we had put into it.

Another time, we were told that the report from the hospital lab came back negative. But then they called back and said there was a mix-up and we were to come in for a valid report.

Then there was the time when a good friend said he would fix the lawn mower by Saturday. But then he called to say he could not do it after all. Later, we learned he went fishing instead.

We thought we had a good, open relationship with someone, and then we heard that he was backstabbing us to others. And when we tried to mend the relationship, we got a cold shoulder.

We had looked up to an older person for years because of his faithfulness. But then he stumbled. Even though we heard he was sorry and corrected his way, it was hard to forget because of how highly we had thought of him.

It is especially difficult when those we depended on and trusted in disappoint us. While we expected them to meet our needs, it became obvious that they needed help themselves. Our disappointment can make us critical and determined to not put confidence in anyone lest we get hurt again.

It's easy to play the "blame game" when we are disappointed. We missed the flight by several minutes. So we blame the long lineup at the security check. Or if that isn't enough, we blame the traffic. That sounds like a friend who told the policeman who stopped him for driving too fast that he was late for a meeting. The policeman had a ready answer: "Mister, you'll just have to leave earlier!"

As you know, there is no end to the list of disappointments we might face. Every disappointment holds the possibility of a negative response. If we let our emotions run at those times, they will get us into deeper trouble.

That is why accepting disappointments is a grace we cannot learn too soon or too well. We want to have free spirits even when things aren't as we wish.

How Can We Deal With Disappointments?

Here are a few suggestions.

Deal with one disappointment at a time. Too many disappointments too close together can eat away at our readiness to dream and look forward. We can become afraid to expect anything. This is because we tend to let our troubles accumulate. Even a broken pencil point can bring tears if we let it be "the straw that broke the camel's back."

Troubles do seem to come in bunches sometimes, as the story of Job confirms. Jesus in the wilderness faced a rush of temptations. We cannot always say, "One problem a week and no more!" But neither should we mentally stack up our problems as if we were making some kind of collection. We can deal with a broken pencil point as just that and no more, even *if* we smashed the car this morning.

Remember to say, "If the Lord will." No, it is not dangerous to say that. Friends of ours had a girl, and then two boys. The girl, who was four or five years old by that time, became eager for a baby sister and prayed for one. Reminded to pray, "If it is Your will," she reluctantly added those words, but in a tiny voice that suggested that she wasn't sure that God was very wise about such important matters. As it turned out, the Lord gave her a sister—eventually, three of them, to her delight.

The Lord is not like the father who automatically says no because—well, just because. Our Father loves to hear our prayers, and He delights in giving us what we ask for unless He has something better in mind. But to truly have freedom, we must be willing to leave the outcome up to Him.

Keep your expectations low-key. We are apt to plan as if we lived in a perfect world and to work toward those plans. But the world is imperfect. There is no certainty that things will work out the way we hope. If we ignore this, we set ourselves up to be disappointed.

One of our neighbors was planning to marry and spent much time preparing their house. Shortly before the wedding, fire gutted the house. His tears flowed as firemen fought the blaze. Another young neighbor's wife took sick and was an invalid a number of years before she passed away. Their life together was not at all what they had planned.

Hoping and planning is fine. Tears of disappointment may be appropriate. But we can keep from being utterly crushed if we remember that life is, after all, uncertain.

Look for healing in acceptance. The witticism "Since I gave up hope, I feel much better" captures this thought. The old saying "What can't be cured can be endured" says something similar. The apostle Peter put it this way: "Forasmuch then as Christ hath suffered for us in the flesh, arm yourselves likewise with the same mind" (1 Peter 4:1). A mind prepared to endure is like a soldier's armor. It doesn't make each day a picnic, but it carries you through.

Don't ever say, "This too shall pass" to someone whose spouse has just died or who has lost an arm in an accident. But if it ever happens to you, remember that in a sense that proverb is actually true. Accepting the loss will, with time and God's help, bring emotional healing, and the acuteness of the pain will pass.

Look for alternatives. Instead of assuming that all is lost, think about other possibilities. If something prevents what you planned to do this evening, use the detour to do something else you have wanted to do. The saying, "It's an ill wind that doesn't blow any good" reminds us to look for something else.

Could it be that God is using this disappointment to steer us in the direction He wants us to go? Looking back, we might be amazed to see that our disappointment worked out for good. Disappointment might be *His*-appointment!

Beware of bitterness. The greater the confidence we place in someone, the greater the disappointment when he fails us. The closer someone is to us, the more it hurts when he turns against us. Jesus faced this in John 13:18, when He said, "He that eateth bread with me hath lifted up his heel against me."

Now suppose someone let us down very badly. We thought we could count on him, but he did not measure up. A crossroads emerges in our relationship. Shall we cross him off our list and have one less friend? No, don't hold a grudge. For if we fail to forgive and be gracious, we will hurt ourselves even more than we hurt other people.

It is so easy to expect more from others than what we expect of ourselves. We fail too. If we expect only from others what we would do at their age and in their circumstances, we will not be disappointed so quickly.

Notice other people who have been disappointed even worse. My father had polio as a child and was lame all his life. During his growing-up years, someone took him to a polio clinic. Later he remarked that he never pitied himself after that because he saw many people there who were much worse off than he.

If your head keeps turning and you see people who seem to have everything, just remember that they have their own problems. God sometimes makes public examples of the rich and famous to communicate this very point.

Submit all your hopes and dreams to the will of God. Yes, it is right to have them. It is right to work to fulfill them. But then, if they don't materialize, leave the whole matter in God's hands. Trust Him. One person, after a severe disappointment, said, "God must have something better!"

The prophet Habakkuk said, "Although the fig tree shall not blossom, neither shall fruit be in the vines; the labour of the olive shall fail, and the fields shall yield no meat; the flock shall be cut off from the fold, and there shall be no herd in the stalls: yet I will rejoice in the LORD, I will joy in the God of my salvation."

Was the prophet asking for all of these calamities to happen? No! But he was saying that if they came, he would still rejoice. That is a serious challenge for us. And when we commit all to the Lord Jesus—even our disappointments—we can then be free indeed!

Chapter Fourteen

Freedom and Disillusionment

We face disillusionment when our bubble of illusion bursts. It comes when the facts intrude on our dream, rudely showing us that our illusion was merely an unrealistic delusion. Disillusionment is dangerous because at the moment the illusion vanishes, our feelings want to slide from the housetop to the basement. They do not stop in the middle, at reality, but go from the best to the worst. The basement of disillusionment is a miserable one.

Two brothers from the Canadian prairies, Abe and Pete, heard how nice it was farther west. From then on, they ate and slept the West. They talked often and enthusiastically about it. To them it was like Canaan; everything was just right. The sales agent showed pictures of loaded fruit trees. Any question about difficulties was brushed aside. They could hardly wait to move.

The time finally came, and the move was made. A local man whose father had hauled their things from the railroad station to their new, out-of-the-way place told me his father felt sorry for the way he "dumped them off in the middle of nowhere."

Well! Things were not as they had thought or dreamed. The climate was much more severe than they had expected. The soil was not what they had imagined it to be. They were disappointed.

Now, the West, in their estimation, became the worst place to be. Abe told me they would have moved away, but they could not, because they were too poor!

That was almost forty years before I met Abe. He had not moved away but still lived in the place he had thought was the best, then the worst, and finally found to be quite tolerable! He had gone full circle and ended up in the middle.

We can act like Abe and Pete about practically anything. When we allow ourselves illusion and then face disillusion, our emotions are in for a rough ride.

Why Do We Create Illusions?

We create illusions because by nature we are not very balanced and we tend to be unable to see the whole picture. We easily fall into the snare of seeing life through the eyes of our feelings. Some days we may feel like we can do everything, and on another day we find it hard to do anything. Things strike us as either all good or all bad. There seems to be no neutral ground between the two extremes.

We can be that way about people. At first we are impressed with them and create an image of them that no mortal could live up to. We think they cannot do anything wrong. After we know them awhile, we may think they can hardly do anything right. Did they really change that much?

Do we create illusions deliberately? Probably a few people do. They prefer living in their make-believe world. One person said she prefers it that way because it is more fun than real life. But most of us do not want to live under illusions, because we know that once the illusion evaporates, hard reality sets in.

Why then do illusions deceive us? Perhaps we fall for or even create illusions because we are given to looking for something better. We hear the sales pitch. We feel the excitement of a challenge. We are sure that whatever the obstacles may be, they will evaporate and disappear and we will achieve what we envision.

Enthusiasm is not all bad. We need it. If we never warmed with enthusiasm, we would tend to only see obstacles and none of the rewards. We might not even want to get out of bed in the morning.

But we need to be aware that by creating illusions, we may be setting ourselves up for some painful eye opening. Let's think what can happen.

From Illusion to Disillusionment

The problem of going from illusion to disillusionment is the distance between the two. We fall too hard. We need a safety net on the same level as reality.

We fall into disillusionment when we start focusing on the negative parts of life. Our days are usually a mix of progress and setback, and usually we move forward more than backward. But if we have had seven hours of progress and one hour of difficulty, which do we remember the quickest? The one-eighth or the seven-eighths?

Disillusionment lies to us. It exaggerates. It blows things out of proportion. It fosters a critical spirit. It militates against faith. It will tell us that there is no one and nothing to believe or trust in. The psalmist himself admitted, "I said in my haste, All men are liars" (Psalm 116:11). Note that he said it in haste!

Disillusionment blinds us to the good there is. It highlights all the negatives until that is all we can see. Things that were barely noticed leap to the forefront.

Husbands have stopped seeing the good in their wives. Wives have stopped seeing the good in their husbands. Some couples, by thinking bad things about each other, have literally thought their way into a difficult marriage. And sadly, some have thought their way right out of their marriage.

Disillusionment spawns a cynical, sarcastic spirit. It destroys relationships. It inflames the emotions with suspicion. It passes strong judgment freely. It leads people to believe their doubts rather than the truth. Some people have become suspicious and doubtful toward a friend, a mentor, or an employer. Once it was all good; now it is all bad.

Disillusionment spoils church life. Some people who have found a new church are enthused at first with everything and think they have found the perfect church. All the churches they have known before are nothing compared with this one. But eventually they become aware of some faults in the newfound group. And if they get out their magnifying glasses, they will be down the road to another church before long.

Not everyone leaves the church when they become disillusioned. Some remain and endure church life, but cannot seem to appreciate the church. They find it easy to complain and criticize. They suspect and surmise about others—and don't keep it to themselves. They do not contribute contentment to the atmosphere. They miss the wonderful blessings of brotherhood that God has for them. And, no doubt, they do more damage to themselves and others than they imagine!

Disillusionment cripples the ability to have faith. It is hard to keep faith in God after we have discredited the faith we had in others. At those times, it is so easy to blame God for how things are. We may blame Him for cheating us out of something we felt entitled to. But no one ever wins when they quarrel with God. No one.

Disillusionment is a cruel place to be. When it takes control of the emotions, we become captives in a cruel prison. How can we escape? and stay free?

From Disillusionment to Reality

Here are a few things we can do to stabilize at the midlevel of reality.

Look up. Our concept of life must be higher than the last bad thing that happened to us. We must build our concepts and convictions on God, not circumstances. Here are some verses to build on.

"Trust in the LORD with all thine heart; and lean not unto thine own understanding. In all thy ways acknowledge him, and he shall direct thy paths" (Proverbs 3:5, 6).

"But the path of the just is as the shining light, that shineth more and more unto the perfect day" (Proverbs 4:18).

"Great peace have they which love thy law: and nothing shall offend them" (Psalm 119:165).

"And we know that all things work together for good to them that love God, to them who are the called according to his purpose" (Romans 8:28).

"There hath no temptation taken you but such as is common to man: but God is faithful, who will not suffer you to be tempted above that ye are able; but will with the temptation also make a way to escape, that ye may be able to bear it" (1 Corinthians 10:13).

Would our emotions swing so widely and wildly if we heeded the truth of these verses?

Be realistic about life. Question your first impressions. Predict the difficulties you will face, and reckon with the uncertainties. You should not be surprised if things turn out differently than you expected. Much of life is that way. You will fall less hard if your expectations are more reasonable.

Practice the Golden Rule. When others fail or disappoint you, give them the same benefit of the doubt you want from them. Don't give up on them just because they failed. Believe in their sincerity as long as you can. The Bible word on this is "Ye have need of patience." Remember how long-suffering God has been to you with your faults.

Take responsibility for your emotions. "The spirits of the prophets are subject to the prophets" (1 Corinthians 14:32). One of the best ways to control your emotions is to control your actions, whether your emotions are high or low. Doing right is always right, whether you feel like it or not. And somehow, it does help to lift the emotions.

Again, we must put our trust in God's love and promises. We must subject our feelings to Him. We need to believe that He has a purpose in all things and that He is indeed able to make good come out of the hard things in life.

Take the psalmist's words to heart: "I had fainted, unless I had believed to see the goodness of the LORD in the land of the living. Wait on the LORD: be of good courage, and he shall strengthen thine heart: wait, I say, on the LORD" (Psalm 27:13, 14).

That is to be free indeed!

Chapter Fifteen

Freedom and Discouragement

As you read the past chapters, you may have noticed that the problems seem to intensify. Disappointment, disillusionment, discouragement (and depression, which follows in the next chapter) are related to each other. If they are allowed to march into our lives and gain supremacy, we cannot have the freedom God wants us to have.

Discouragement is disappointment and disillusionment gone to seed. Discouragement affects one's outlook, like an extremely dark pair of sunglasses. Even though the causes of discouragement are often real, discouragement is often an overreaction to unfavorable circumstances. A few years before the Wright brothers flew their first airplane, one of them was so discouraged after another unsuccessful attempt, that he remarked, "Man will fly, but not for a hundred years."

According to the lore of frontier life, in eastern Oregon, during the covered-wagon migrations to the West, a group of pioneers ran out of water and died of thirst. The record left was chipped into a rock with the date 1856. One of the saddest parts about it was that those people were within seeing distance of a river but they did not know it. They gave up just before they got there!

Here is another illustration.

Amos watched his son Aaron out of the corner of his eye. Aaron was standing in the corner of the church, looking dejected and forlorn.

"Aaron, what was wrong at church tonight?" his father questioned him later. "I noticed earlier that you were so quiet. And then at church I saw you stand around as if you had lost your last friend."

Aaron slouched deeper into the sofa. "That's how I feel. I thought Joshua and I were good friends. Even though he is much older than I and has been such a help to me, it's over. You remember how he ignored me several months ago when I called him? He never returned my call. When I thought back over it, I knew it wasn't the first time. He's let me down so many times! And when I saw him visiting with Robert tonight, I figured it's over. I don't think I'll ever try to have a friend again," he finished, cupping his head in his hands.

"Now, son, take courage. Are you sure it's that bad?" his father comforted. "You can try again." But Aaron shook his head wearily.

That is discouragement—the loss of courage and optimism. Obstacles loom like mountain walls that nothing seems able to penetrate.

How Discouragement Affects Our Freedom

Discouragement makes life look overwhelming. It makes the present problems look insurmountable. It makes us feel like the spies who described the inhabitants of Canaan, saying, "We were like grasshoppers in their sight." That would be over fifty times bigger than they! Were they really that big? Hardly, but that is how they felt!

Discouragement blocks out the hope of change. A lot of things can be lost in life, but few losses are as serious as losing hope. Hope is one of the brightest spots in our souls. It is like light at the end of the tunnel or like the silver linings of the clouds. It keeps our spirits up. If that light is snuffed out, we are in serious trouble.

Discouragement is persistent. Someone moved into a new community and set about to make a good garden. The soil was poor, so he brought in manure. A neighbor looked across the fence and said, "You're putting too much manure on."

The soil was heavy, so the new owner brought in sand. The neighbor looked across the fence and said, "You're putting in too much sand."

Finally harvesttime came. The new owner dug potatoes—big potatoes. He saw the neighbor looking across the fence and showed him one of his prizes. By now, he had an idea what the neighbor would say, and sure enough he said it: "Cut it in half. I'm almost positive it's hollow."

Discouragement undermines our confidence in others. We measure them by how we feel about ourselves. It breeds suspicion of people and their motives. It becomes hard to believe that they mean well and that they care about us. We end up feeling terribly alone.

Discouragement erodes confidence in ourselves and our ability to solve problems. It whispers to us that if we try, we will only make things worse. Indeed, if we allow ourselves to follow that train of thought, we will make matters worse.

Worst of all, ***discouragement affects our outlook toward God.*** It affects our confidence in His goodness. We find it hard to agree with the poet when he said, "Behind a frowning providence / He hides a smiling face."

Who can praise God when he is discouraged? Who is thankful? I remember the time we sat waiting in an airplane on the end of the runway. We were fogged in, held captive by low, heavy clouds. The pilot said we couldn't fly away until the clouds broke open and let us out. That is how our spirits are when we are discouraged. We are locked in. We can't fly!

When courage is lost, we become afraid of everything. Bushes and stumps look like crouching bears. Even our own shadows are frightening.

Discouragement leads us to make unfair comparisons. The psalmist said, in Psalm 73:2, 3, "But as for me, my feet were almost gone; my steps had well nigh slipped. For I was envious at the foolish, when I saw the prosperity of the wicked." When he finally went into the house of God and thought about the end of the wicked, he got his feet on solid ground again.

Discouragement blames others unfairly. David and his men had gone to battle and left their wives and children in the city of Ziklag. While they were gone, enemies came and took their wives and children, and burned their city. When David and his men returned, they were devastated. No wonder! All was lost. The Bible says, "Then David and the people that were with him lifted up their voice and wept, until they had no more power to weep" (1 Samuel 30:4).

David's men did what people often do when they get discouraged. They then turned on David, blamed him, and threatened to stone him.

According to 1 Samuel 30:6, David was greatly discouraged. How do we know? Because we are told how he handled the situation. "But David encouraged himself in the LORD his God." This brings us to our next point.

Escaping Discouragement

We must truly want to be free if we hope to escape discouragement. Some people want to get away from discouragement—sometime. But they are not quite done pitying themselves. Maybe they would like to punish someone for a while yet.

We must want to avoid becoming discouraged in the first place. The old saying, "A stitch in time saves nine," holds good here. Once we recognize the symptoms, we can take preventive steps. Like a cold, discouragement is more easily stopped in its early stages than later on. Or, discouragement can be like getting sleepy while driving. We need to nip it in the bud. One person who drove a good bit said he never fell asleep at the wheel while he was fighting sleep. But when he ignored the symptoms of sleepiness, then he was in grave danger.

We must be as persistent as discouragement is, turning our back on it every time it makes another suggestion.

Don't let the little things get you down. Looking back, were you ever amazed at how little it took to upset your cart? The Bible says that it is "the little foxes that spoil the vines."

Little hindrances can multiply at incredible speed. When the French tried to build a canal across Panama, they were not stopped by high mountains and flowing rivers. They were stopped by pesky mosquitoes that spread yellow fever. When the tiny mosquitoes were conquered in the next undertaking, then the canal could be built.

Watch for the telltale signs. Beware when you feel gloomy and unmotivated, or when you feel impatient toward others. Beware when everyone around you seems dispirited, for we often see in others what we are frustrated about in ourselves.

Backtrack if necessary. Don't be afraid to look back and see where things started downhill. Don't make excuses; just learn from your mistakes.

Be realistic. Resist the temptation to enjoy believing your own lies. Are things really as bad as they look? Are they as bad as your feelings are telling you?

Coming back to David, how did he encourage himself in the Lord? Quite likely, he looked back over his life and traced God's past faithfulness to him. There were many evidences of how good God had been to him. He probably rehearsed God's promises from the past and for the future. And then he realized that God had promises for the present too. He was aware of unfulfilled prophecies concerning himself in the kingdom of Israel. And he realized that God was not done with him.

He must have concluded that God was with him and would not fail him now. So he took steps forward, asking guidance from the Lord. Then he persuaded his discouraged men to take courage and go with him to battle. His encouragement worked.

What can you and I do to take courage? Many similar things, and more. We have the Word of God, where we can find examples, admonition, direction, and strength. The Holy Spirit is in us to guide us into all truth. We usually have nearby brothers and sisters in Christ to help us. Don't neglect to seek them out.

We need to keep our immune system healthy. Spiritual immunity determines whether every "bug" that comes around will find a cozy nest within us where it can multiply. We may need to spend more time seeking God in the Bible, in prayer, and in meditation. One man who was discouraged took his Bible and hymnbook and went off by himself. He was blessed!

So, dear friend, take courage. God is still on the throne. His plans for us will blossom if we are faithful to Him. Read the promises to the overcomers in the letters to the seven churches in Revelation 2 and 3. Determine, by the grace of God, to be among the overcomers.

Claim this promise from Jude 24 and 25: "Now unto him that is able to keep you from falling, and to present you faultless before the presence of his glory with exceeding joy, to the only wise God our Saviour, be glory and majesty, dominion and power, both now and ever. Amen."

And don't forget to claim this promise of Jesus: "If the Son therefore shall make you free, ye shall be free indeed." Free to take courage and go on!

Chapter
Sixteen

Freedom and Depression

*"Bring my soul out of prison,
that I may praise thy name" (Psalm 142:7).*

Depression has been called the common cold of emotional difficulties because many people are affected by it to some degree. Since depression is so common, believers need to think about how to deal with it as God intended.

Depression is also like the common cold in that it comes in so many forms and varying degrees of intensity. Most people use the term *depression* quite loosely. It can range from a melancholy feeling of sadness to an indescribable depth of despair. Whatever shape or form it comes in, those who have been there know that depression is not enjoyable. No doubt, depression can become much more acute than the common cold. It can seem more like double pneumonia. It becomes a thief that robs the soul of its joy in the Lord.

In this chapter, we will search for Bible answers to this human problem. This chapter does not pose as a fix-it clinical treatment of depression with a set of one-two-three answers. It is intended to help identify some causes, symptoms, and warning signals that can give insight into how depression works. It offers sympathy, encouragement, and hope, because we believe God does have ways to help us have peace and joy in our souls.

Describing Depression

The term *depression* describes a variety of emotional experiences, such as sadness, sorrow, heavy-heartedness, gloom, despair, or lethargic weariness. Often we call these feelings the blues. We should make a difference, however, between passing feelings and those that settle in and take up residence with us.

Depression is one of the "basements" of emotional life. The disappointment, disillusionment, and discouragement of the three previous chapters have not only gone to seed but now have also taken root and dug themselves into our system. Like noxious plants, their roots spread and gain a tenacious hold over the soul.

In Psalm 142, the psalmist called depression a prison! He described it like this: "I poured out my complaint before him; I shewed before him my trouble. When my spirit was overwhelmed within me . . ." (verses 2, 3). His spirit was faint, and his courage was gone. Life was too big for him. That was why he begged in verse 7, "Bring my soul out of prison."

Those who have been there know the feeling. Someone described it as being out on the ocean with no one to help. Another said it is like being in a deep, deep pit, where no one can reach you. The dictionary calls it "prolonged feelings of despair and dejection." These sensations are entrenched; they involve more than mere passing feelings.

Some who have suffered depression say it is like being in a long, dark tunnel with no light ahead to bring hope that it will end. In reality, the light may be just around the next bend in the tunnel; but if you have ever been in that kind of darkness, then you know that one of the most depressing things about depression is that life seems totally hopeless. If you could see some light—some hope that, down the road, the trial will end—then it might be bearable. But when no light is seen ahead and there is no way out, then life seems impossible.

Depression is to humans what the Great Depression was to the world economy in the 1930s. Business stalled, causing job losses. Money devalued and was almost worthless. Property values plummeted. Consumer confidence in the banking system bottomed out so badly that the banks had to close because people made a run to get their money out before it got worse. Employment was so scarce that there was little money to be earned or spent. Poverty prevailed. The generation who lived through that time never forgot its hardships.

Suicide was common in those days. Men hurled themselves off buildings when they saw their fortunes evaporate and all that they trusted in was gone.

The Great Depression did not come overnight. It followed the Roaring Twenties as the result of a gradual slide with early, ominous warnings that were not heeded. In spite of much political maneuvering and attempted cures during those years, it seems to have taken World War II to get money moving again. And yet, it took the world a whole decade to climb back out!

Human depression does the same. Even though it is largely an emotional condition, it affects the whole person. When the emotions take someone through the dark, dismal valleys and over hills of depression, they affect the whole body. The pain and incapacities become as real as a broken leg.

The emotions can also wrap themselves around the spiritual part of a person and block out the sunlight of God. They shroud His promises and make Him seem far away. Faith becomes difficult because everything looks so dark. The emotions become stronger than the will and thus hold the person captive.

Some personalities are more vulnerable to depression than others. Some people are more optimistic by nature. They see opportunities where others see only obstacles. Others take the daily ups and downs of life more seriously than they ought. Those who are on the pessimistic side need to be extra alert to the possibility of depression.

Even highly productive and useful people are candidates for depression. The emotional intensity with which they work, the sensitivity that enables them to connect and enter into the experiences of others, and the concentrated meditating they do puts a heavy strain on their emotional system. These people need to learn to work within the framework of their emotional constitution.

Depression is usually most easily noticed in how we feel emotionally. But it can also affect us physically in ways we might not think about. The emotions can cast a net over the whole body that affects a person's energy level. Here's how it can work:

Normally, Arthur was an unusually productive man. He dived into his work with great zeal. He gave himself to evangelistic work unreservedly. But now he was struggling, discouraged, and miserable. Instead of being optimistic and energetic, everything looked dark and foreboding. What was usually a pleasure became a burden. He was so tired that he ended up in bed because he could barely move. He was sure he was going to die. He kept taking his pulse because he expected his heart to stop any minute. On one of his bad days, it was time to butcher chickens for market. He was sure he couldn't do it, and informed his wife he couldn't get up, because he was sure he was going to die that day.

We'll tell the rest of the story later. For now, it describes how depression can work. There are cases of less intensity but similar pain.

Depression can come in mild, moderate, or major forms. Some people susceptible to depression tend to swing from one extreme to the other. They reach an extreme high where feelings of invincibility surge and nothing seems impossible. They can do anything and everything. Then they hit a low, where everything feels impossible and they become extremely sad. Either way, feeling or fantasy replaces fact.

Just as we may identify trees by their fruit, we want to examine this difficulty by its fruit.

Early Warnings of Depression

Why do people become seriously depressed? A broad answer may be that they ignore the early warnings. Failure to try to understand them opens the door to more difficulty. Like most sicknesses, they are more easily remedied if identified in their early stages.

We should not be worrying as soon as we don't feel just right. We simply won't always feel as if we are on top of the world. The symptoms we are going to point out can be looked at as danger signals only if they persist. However, the quicker they are recognized and dealt with, the better.

Emotions can be compared to various things. Vehicle tires can have a slow air leak. If we keep refilling the tire until we get it fixed, it is a mere inconvenience. But if we don't keep filling it, we will ruin it.

One man had back problems, but he wanted to finish his work at the sawmill for the season before he tended to it. By that time, the damage was far more extensive than it would have been if he had been treated earlier.

An extensive departure from one's usual disposition can be a warning. A person needs to be measured against his normal self rather than against others. If those who are normally quiet become aggressive, and the more active become passive, it is worth noticing. Or perhaps those who are usually buoyant become constantly sad, or the normally sober become too happy. If things that usually don't bother us become a burden, it too can be a warning signal.

Depression can cause a tendency to withdraw from others. Even the efforts of others to comfort and encourage the depressed one are pushed aside and rejected. Kind words are rebuffed with caustic answers or silence. The hood of self-pity is drawn more tightly about the head. The person rejects what he may need the most.

Another symptom of depression is a lack of motivation. Nothing seems worth doing. The emotions have a "soul in prison" feeling. The spirit is stifled, and the emotions feel pressed and weighted down. The person feels like a tire without air. The zest and inspiration for living are gone. If anything needs to be done, it looks impossible. The things that usually produced excitement are dull and drab.

The inability to "feel" thankful and joyful often accompanies depression. When the sunshine seems gray and nothing is good, and when God doesn't seem to do anything right for us, trouble is lurking.

The body can be affected in varying ways. For some it is sleeplessness. The body refuses to shut down and relax. However, others want to do nothing but sleep. (Here again, comparing present behavior with normal patterns can shed light on this.) Either way, the reservoir of energy becomes depleted.

The loss of spiritual vision is a serious symptom because of the toll it takes on us spiritually. When God seems far away and trouble seems near, it robs us of peace and confidence in Him. The psalmist must have had that feeling when he cried out, in Psalm 27:9, "Hide not thy face from me; put not thy servant away in anger: thou hast been my help; leave me not, neither forsake me, O God of my salvation."

Another obvious symptom of depression may be lack of emotional control. The emotions become irrational and refuse to respond to the person's will. Ideas about one's own abilities may soar to great heights or sink to miserable lows. Ideas about others can become warped. It then seems that the other people are acting strangely—or at least triggering how the depressed person feels and what he does. He might feel like the person who said, "I am the only one who has his head screwed on straight."

These symptoms are real and need to be reckoned with. But we want to search behind them and try to see some causes. For it is good to recognize the causes and to remedy them beforehand—like putting a guardrail at the top of the hill rather than an ambulance at the bottom!

Causes of Depression

We could ask why believers are troubled with depression. Should not our walk with the Lord spare us from such turmoil? Should not our emotions easily be subject to us?

Part of the answer lies in the fact that our humanity is subject to pressure. We are touched by our surroundings, the people we associate with, and all the experiences of life. There are choices and decisions to make. There are competitions for our loyalties on every hand. We have our own nature to deal with. And Satan is constantly trying to take advantage of us.

In the midst of it all, we are called to a life of balance and holiness. That is why Paul prayed, in 1 Thessalonians 5:23, “And the very God of peace sanctify you wholly; and I pray God your whole spirit and soul and body be preserved blameless unto the coming of our Lord Jesus Christ.”

Believers are normally sensitive people—and should be. We take life seriously. We try to respond to life as we ought. We have our own particular emotions, burdens, and problems to deal with. Yet we get involved with the needs of others because we care about them too. When things don’t go well for them, we empathize with their pain and sorrow.

While we are trying to help others, several things can happen. Sometimes we are greatly helped ourselves. On the other hand, we need to be careful that we don’t slip into the ditch when trying to pull someone else out.

Let’s consider some other common causes.

Unresolved sin has caused depression often enough that it is usually suspected first. We know that if sin is not brought under the cleansing power of the blood of Jesus by proper repentance, it will cause problems. But thanks be to God that He made it possible for us to be forgiven and redeemed from sin and set free from its power! If sin is the problem, help needs to be sought by repentance and faith in the Lord Jesus Christ. Then we can move on to other possible causes.

An unresolved conflict may be haunting the mind. It may be an accident liability or a potential lawsuit. It may be an unhappy neighbor. An acquaintance who owns livestock says that his neighbor keeps calling the environmentalists because of his animals. When the list of such matters gets too long, they become a burden on the emotions.

Our emotions are like a bank account. We must maintain funds equal to what we draw out, or we will be in trouble. Our emotional batteries need to stay charged. Our bodies are like that too. They require a certain amount of rest to fulfill given duties because the debt of overtaxed emotions can cause depression and take their toll physically.

Circumstances, such as bank accounts, can affect the emotions. Yesterday a man said he spent the day paying bills, and he was getting depressed. Apparently there was a connection between his bank account and his emotional level.

A man's wife reported yesterday that her husband is so busy at work he is becoming depressed. Three phone calls waiting and a customer at the counter can be too much for most people. Some people thrive on pressure, while others wear away under it. For some, not being busy enough is depressing. Everyone needs to find his working level.

Emotions can become overloaded, burned out, and broken down—even while we are immersed in doing good things. Arthur, the man we noted earlier, could not keep his demanding pace and collapsed in bed.

An unusual drain on the emotions can bring on depression. This emotional depletion can come by such things as the prolonged pressure of sickness (our own or those close to us), or the suffering or death of a loved one, or a move to a strange location. The drain may be so gradual that the process is nearly imperceptible.

This can happen when too many changes come too close together. They are sometimes called bumps in the road. Last night while rounding a curve on a hill, my compact car lost its footing and vibrated toward the ditch because the pavement had a series of cracks close together. That can happen emotionally if we are not careful.

Disappointment can do the same to us. John the Baptist preached fearlessly with conviction that Jesus was the Messiah. Then when John ended up in prison, he began to wonder about Jesus' ministry (and maybe his own). He sent his disciples to ask Jesus, "Art thou he that should come, or do we look for another?" (Matthew 11:3). He asked a question about something he had been very sure about before. Now he spoke the language of the struggling soul whose faith is eclipsed.

Impatience is akin to disappointment. Like John the Baptist, when Jesus' ministry did not work out as John had expected, we may wonder why our hopes and dreams do not materialize. We have earnestly sought the Lord. Why then do we wait in vain for His answer?

Depression can be caused by a trapped feeling of powerlessness to change the present distressful situation. It can overshadow a mother in the home, the husband at his work, or a child about his home. Even a youth, who is usually optimistic by nature, might look into the future and feel like a victim rather than an overcomer. The sad statistics of suicide rates at this age show how powerful depression can be.

Physical, biological, and hormonal changes can stress the emotions. Childbearing creates far-reaching stresses that should receive sympathetic consideration. Biological upsets occur for many of us and need to be reckoned with.

Unthankfulness and discontentment contribute to depression. Self-centeredness and self-pity are bound to set in. They are cruel masters and terrible tenants in our emotional system.

Loneliness because of isolation can cause depression. In the North Country, when the hard winter locks people into their houses, they say they have cabin fever. They have no hope of escaping by going elsewhere, and they have no hope of anyone coming to them.

Oddly, people can feel just as isolated and just as lonely when they are among many people. Social, or "soul," isolation can cause people to despair because they feel they have no one to reach out to. There are many sad stories of what people have done to themselves and others because of it.

Last but not least, one's own personal life might seem worthless because of not feeling needed by anyone. When there is nothing to live for, nothing to look forward to, nothing to trust in, and no one who cares, something gives way.

We could sum up most of these causes by saying they are poor or wrong responses to the circumstances of life. Somewhere, someone has missed the path and allowed himself to be taken down another way.

Whatever the cause, depression is cruel. Let's see how it can work.

The Clutches of Depression

It's hard to put descriptions like this on paper because of how painful depression is. But pondering the slippery slopes of depression will help us be more alert to the early stages of sliding.

Depression clutches its victims and then pulls them downward. It heaps misery on misery. It amplifies and magnifies all the things that need to be done: the grass needs to be mowed, the garden needs to be weeded, the kitchen is a mess, the shop needs to be cleaned, and the barn chores are way behind. Whatever it is, it looks overwhelming. And it hangs on—and grows!

The clutches can become so strong that the mind can hardly think rationally. We must recognize that our minds, like our bodies, have their limits. Depression greatly lowers the ability to cope.

Depression is cruel. When it rules, it becomes like a cold, stone castle prison with the drawbridges pulled up, the windows blocked shut, and the doors securely locked. Escape seems impossible. The only future is more of the same misery. It makes the possibility of help seem hopeless. No one understands; no one cares. And even if they would, there is nothing they can do. Worse yet, does God care?

These clutches can become so powerful that death seems more welcome than life. Is that how Elijah felt when he begged God, "It is enough; now, O LORD, take away my life" (1 Kings 19:4)?

One of the saddest and most urgent aspects of depression is its ability to take people to the brink of despair—to the point of self-destruction. Although we will never know all the facts on this, we can learn from the few who have come back from the edge and told us about it.

One of these was William Cowper, who was haunted with deep melancholia. He wrote the familiar song, "God Moves in a Mysterious Way." It is thought to be one of his final hymns and to be a reflection of God's leading throughout his own lifetime. Supposedly, he wrote it after an unsuccessful attempt at suicidal drowning.

This is what he said:

God moves in a mysterious way,
  His wonders to perform;
He plants His footsteps in the sea,
  And rides upon the storm.

Ye fearful saints, fresh courage take;
The clouds ye so much dread
Are big with mercy, and shall break
In blessings on your head.

Judge not the Lord by feeble sense,
But trust Him for His grace;
Behind a frowning providence
He hides a smiling face.

Blind unbelief is sure to err,
And scan His work in vain;
God is His own interpreter,
And He will make it plain.

We are glad Mr. Cowper found the "right" answer and took the better road.

The temptation to suicide may sound like a worst-case scenario that few Christians need to face. Hopefully it is. However, there are those who have come back from the brink—and are living testimonies that even the worst of depression can be overcome. Praise God! They are back because they rested in God and found new assurance that God cares. And He has answers for us, both practical and spiritual.

Finding the Way Out of Depression

Let's start from God's side. God gave us many evidences of concern for those in depressed situations.

Think about Elijah. God didn't let him die as he asked. Instead, He gave him sleep and then sent an angel with food. Then again Elijah slept. "And the angel of the LORD came again the second time, and touched him, and said,

Arise and eat; because the journey is too great for thee." What gentle mercy! "And he arose, and did eat and drink, and went in the strength of that meat forty days and forty nights unto Horeb the mount of God" (1 Kings 19:7, 8).

Think how Jesus wept for the pain of others. Read in Luke 4:18 about the people Jesus said He came to help—especially the poor, the brokenhearted, the captives, the blind, and the bruised. Listen to Jesus when He says, in Matthew 11:28, "Come unto me, all ye that labour and are heavy laden, and I will give you rest." That includes rest from depression!

Jesus had a mixed message for the two disciples on the Emmaus road. First He said, in Luke 24:17, "What manner of communications are these that ye have one to another, as ye walk, and are sad?" He knew that everyone suffers disappointment and discouragement in life. He knew why and how they felt.

Later in the conversation with the two, Jesus spoke very forthrightly. He said, in verses 25–27, "O fools, and slow of heart to believe all that the prophets have spoken. . . . And beginning at Moses and all the prophets, he expounded unto them in all the scriptures the things concerning himself."

These Scriptures show that Jesus is always eager to lift up the downcast. He not only sympathizes but He also helps. Does He have any idea what these things are like? Hebrews 4:15 assures us He does: "For we have not an high priest which cannot be touched with the feeling of our infirmities; but was in all points tempted like as we are, yet without sin."

Consider the way Jesus dealt with John the Baptist's question when he began to doubt. Did He scold him? or humiliate him? No. Jesus just told his disciples to stay around for a while. "Jesus answered and said unto them,

Go and shew John again those things which ye do hear and see: the blind receive their sight, and the lame walk, the lepers are cleansed, and the deaf hear, the dead are raised up, and the poor have the gospel preached to them. And blessed is he, whosoever shall not be offended in me" (Matthew 11:4–6).

When we read between the lines of that answer, it is clear that Jesus was gently leading John back to his former conviction and confidence. What encouragement!

Talking about practical helps is like going to a nutritionist for help with a physical problem. Quite likely, he will take a broad approach that will cover a multitude of possible deficiencies. He will prescribe a number of things, hoping at least that some of his nutrients will be on target. Likewise, since we human beings have varied needs, our suggestions will be wide-ranging, with the hope that encouragement and help will be found for those in depression and for those who are trying to help others.

We don't want to be like someone telling a driver at the scene of a serious accident how he should have prevented it all! Neither do we want to oversimplify the depression problem to the point that sufferers become even more depressed. Sometimes would-be comforters glibly say, "Have faith in God." It is easy to think that if depressed people believed in the goodness of God, their problems would be solved. And that if they took our advice (and maybe their own advice from time past), things would turn around quickly. Anything less than that is considered the long way around.

But those in depression often discover that it may not be that simple, even though they wish it were. Interestingly, depression can serve as a school from which a sufferer can learn valuable things. Sometimes we too can learn from people who are or have been depressed.

A step toward being helped is to recognize and accept the problem of depression. Many of us are reluctant to go see a doctor about physical problems. We put it off because we want to get better by ourselves—and that's good if it works. However, sometimes trying to get better emotionally before getting help can stretch out the problem.

Recognizing depression can be difficult and painful—especially when it is viewed as an evidence of weakness and inferiority or of an unresolved spiritual problem. This is especially so when a person's circle of friends treats it that way and when people distance themselves from the afflicted one. We, however, should not be that way! If a person ever needs friends, it is at a time like this. The brotherhood of believers ought to be a real place of refuge and encouragement.

Might depression be like an overload switch in a motor, which shuts it down before worse damage is done? Might it be like my friend who lost control of his loaded log truck at the top of a hill? He said he ditched it right at the top lest he have a much worse wreck at the bottom. Although we may not look at a shutdown or a breakdown as a friendly thing, it could be just that—if it saves us from something worse to come.

One person who sought help gave two powerful pieces of advice.

First, find someone you can be totally honest with, and feel free to tell him exactly how you feel. This kind of person will listen and honestly try to understand. He will not be afraid of feeling the hurt. He must know God and be ready to point you to Him while he, as a fellow human, walks beside you in the ups and downs. He must care enough to accept some resistance and abuse, and will not quickly write you off. He must be someone who believes in you when you don't believe in yourself—someone who has faith when you have a hard time having faith—someone who keeps taking you to the facts rather than to your feelings—someone who assures you of the presence of God. He must be someone who will stand up to you and hold you accountable for as much as you can bear.

Hardly anything is more valuable during such times than a bosom friend and companion in Christ. But be very selective about whom you talk to. Limit your talk to those who can keep confidential information and can be trusted to use what you tell them wisely. Matters are not helped by spreading your problem too far, because later you will wish you hadn't. It will only make the way back harder.

Second, don't make irreversible decisions while depressed. Make only the decisions that need to be made. Get help with those decisions from friends who are trustworthy. Some people decide to quit their jobs and to move to another community. Some decide that their church is not helping them enough or is wrong in some other way, so they decide to move on. Some sell their animals to have less work. One depressed man became determined to sell his property. He begged someone to buy it to lighten his load. Later, he felt bad because the people he sold it to were not inclined to return it to him when he felt better!

Again, it is better to trust the judgment of others in times of depression. Those who have gone through deep waters had to learn to trust others more than their own feelings. When God seemed far away, they had to be told—and told again—that He loved them. Even though the Bible seemed flat and dry, they had to be told to believe it. They had to be spoon-fed with the simple truths from it. Even though anxiety and self-pity tried to crowd their minds, slowly but surely the healing process happened. Every day became a marvel, a day for God!

One urgent sign of needing help is being plagued with suicidal thoughts. They are indeed dangerous because they suggest murder—which is what taking one's own life is. Satan maintains that this is the way out of the present trouble, but he doesn't show the eternal trouble it causes. If these thoughts persist, help should be sought—immediately.

That raises the question of where to go for help. We are not talking here about professional counselors and psychiatrists. Help is usually much closer home than that. Help lies in mature people around you who give evidence of knowing God and the way He works in people. They might not have fancy book answers, but if they have caring hearts, they can point a struggling person in the right direction.

It doesn't take professional degrees to help the depressed. It takes love—deep, deep love—love that only God can give. The family of believers is the place to look for this kind of love. You may find it in the pastor, the janitor, a mother with a baby on her lap, a friend here or there, or someone with no title at all. You may find it in a budding believer whose heart desires to grow. That person may even have struggles of his own, but that doesn't matter if he wants to be a vessel for the Lord and embodies the love of God.

The brotherhood of believers needs to sense its responsibility to minister to this kind of need. Although it may seem hard to know exactly what to do, the outstretched arms of love enveloping the struggling one can do more than we can imagine. Rather than standing by critically, love . . . and love some more. Even though it may seem but a cup of cold water, if it is done in the Name of the

Lord, it has heaven's blessing on it. And likely, it will be received as such.

Here are a few things to remember when trying to help someone. Be patient and charitable as a "minister of God." Remember that the person does not want to be where he is, and does not enjoy his present state any more than we would, even if he seems to afflict himself.

Be ready to absorb some accusations as the person ventilates his feelings. Don't accept his charges toward you or others as being factual, because it is a troubled person's viewpoint. Don't counterattack or try to vindicate yourself on every score or even to fix the blame at the moment. When things return to normal, you will be glad you didn't.

Sometimes depressed persons need tough advice. Love is not always soft and easy. A depressed person may need to be told what he doesn't want to hear. He may not appreciate the demands placed upon him. The help may seem unsympathetic and even cruel, but there can be therapeutic value in this.

We can learn from a doctor's manner with his patients. While he exercises gentleness and grace, he must also use candidness, frankness, and honesty, even if it doesn't always sound so nice. There is a time for kid gloves, but they can't always be used when one is up against a larger problem. Doctors have usually have found a balance that we can learn from.

Remember Arthur, who thought he was going to die on butchering day? Do you know what brought him around? He said his wife told him (and this was his own testimony), "If you are going to die today, you may as well do it in the chicken coop. Let's go."

He went to the chicken coop that day and lived to tell the story for many years! That day God gave his wife the wisdom to know what to say; it was what he needed!

There are others we can learn from. One person was seriously injured in an accident, and recovery was very slow. The tendency to despondency was strong. After two years, he was still not fully recovered. But he said one thing helped him: counting his blessings.

Thankfulness is a positive step in finding the way out. Depression is primarily negative. Everything looks bad. But when you focus attention on what is good, you will see more and more good things. Think of things to praise God for. Follow the example of Psalm 119:164: "Seven times a day do I praise thee because of thy righteous judgments." Then the difficulties do not seem as bad.

The way out of depression requires sorting through priorities. Many times the way into depression was paved by twisted priorities that produced unthankfulness. Some things became more important than they should have while others were neglected. At these times, emotional restoration requires postponement of some things until another time. Don't we all find relief from our to-do lists when we figure out why some things don't need to be done now?

One of the hard lessons to learn is to recognize our own limitations. We may need to say no if saying yes overtaxes our ability to be effective. For the time being, we may need to lay aside what we think others expect of us. The desire to have everyone's approval and admiration is a crushing load to bear.

In the search for priorities, we may discover we had some selfish goals. We may have desired acceptance and praise from others. We may have sought recognition for achievement. We may have been driven by some personal ambition. Suddenly all we worked toward lies at our feet as smoking rubble. Then what? The only way out is to come back penitently to the cross for new priorities and new power.

There have been amazing changes for the better in the lives of some who went through times of depression. They have proven that it does not need to be a lifelong debilitation. They gained a deeper, more spiritual perspective of life while they were down. They became more mellow before their Maker. They wanted to live more singularly for the Master. God had new horizons for them in their walk with Him.

Patient contentment is an anchor for the soul. At times we need to be satisfied with the way things are. However, we may bring our apprehensions and fears to the Lord; He invites us to do so. "Casting all your care upon him; for he careth for you" (1 Peter 5:7).

Perfectionists can vex themselves tremendously at the thought of their own imperfections. They may need to learn to be satisfied with being less than superhuman. Their hopes or dreams may need to be put on hold and committed to God. Freedom is found by letting those things go that God has not chosen to give us.

Depression often carries a lot of baggage from the past, such as painful memories, failures, remorse. In the first place, all sin has to be brought to the foot of the cross and washed away in the blood of Jesus. Then those memories need to be put among the things the apostle Paul mentioned in Philippians 3:13: "Forgetting those things which are behind, and reaching forth unto those things which are before." Thank God we can be free from those things of the past!

A major cure for depression is to surrender everything to God. It may seem like a paradox, but strong-willed people often find it hard to accept undesirable things. They continue to fight them in their minds. But until everything is let go but God, nothing else works.

Depression often shows a critical spirit. It is easy to see the faults of others. It is easy to compare their favored positions with our own. But the only way to freedom from this critical spirit is to leave everything and everyone else in God's hands and not feel we have the right to be their critic and judge. It is better "to live and let live."

Sometimes we concern ourselves about what others should be doing. When Peter asked Jesus what John was to do, Jesus had an answer that still works today: "What is that to thee? Follow thou me" (John 21:22). Freedom comes by concentrating on our relationship with God and not on others. One person was told that most of the trouble he had was not his; he was concerning himself about things that were none of his business.

Some physical helps are worth considering. The listlessness of depression produces laziness. Physical exercise and exertion are good and can also help the problem of sleeplessness. Vigorous exercise and sweet rest go together. Ecclesiastes 5:12 tells us that sleep is sweet to the tired body. Exercise and proper rest contribute to the general well-being of our whole person.

Giving attention to diet and nutritional intake is helpful because our health is affected by what we eat and drink. Although some people give undue attention to their diet, other people wish they had paid more attention to their health earlier.

Sometimes people wonder if a depressed person should get medical help (or should stop getting it). One could raise many questions in this area, which we are not qualified to address. On the other hand, most medical doctors are not qualified to deal with all the issues that spiritual people consider important. It may be helpful to draw from their knowledge and medication. However, their methods dare not interfere with Bible directives and threaten our spiritual lives in any way.

As we have moved through these varied suggestions, they all point in one direction—to God. He is the only source of real help!

The only hand that can pull us up out of depression is God's. Can't we feel Him reaching down? He is saying, "Put your hand into Mine. I love you. I will hold you; I will help you. Trust Me." For a person who is not depressed, this may sound simple. For a person who is depressed, it may sound hard. Either way, God's promise is true!

God has promised to answer and open His door to those who ask, seek, and knock. At times, depressed people must do what they may not feel like doing—like reading the Bible and praying—not just every now and again. It may take discipline and effort. Just remember that eating food may take effort sometimes too. But that doesn't keep it from being good for us.

The spiritual man must be fed. He must be built up by feeding on the Word. Jude 20 and 21 gives us this direction: "But ye, beloved, building up yourselves on your most holy faith, praying in the Holy Ghost, keep yourselves in the love of God, looking for the mercy of our Lord Jesus Christ unto eternal life."

Anchor yourself in the Word of God. Its value to the soul cannot be measured. The following powerful poem is good for all of us.

God's Unchanging Word

For feelings come and feelings go,
And feelings are deceiving.
My warrant is the Word of God;
Naught else is worth believing.

Though all my heart should feel condemned
For want of some sweet token,
There is One greater than my heart
Whose Word cannot be broken.

I'll trust in God's unchanging Word
Till soul and body sever;
For though all things shall pass away,
His Word shall stand forever.

—*Martin Luther*

We started this section by pointing the depressed to God. We come back to that again by letting two people who have passed through deep waters speak to us.

The psalmist was deeply troubled in Psalm 42. He poured out his heart like this: "O my God, my soul is cast down within me. . . . all thy waves and thy billows are gone over me" (verses 6, 7). But after seeking God, he said, "Why art thou cast down, O my soul? and why art thou disquieted within me? hope in God: for I shall yet praise him, who is the health of my countenance" (43:5). He found his way out of the deep by coming to God.

The apostle Paul tells about a time "that we were pressed out of measure, above strength, insomuch that we despaired even of life" (2 Corinthians 1:8). That sounds like a depressing situation. He goes on to tell how they trusted not in themselves, "but in God which raiseth the dead."

Here are two more promises.

"Wait on the LORD: be of good courage, and he shall strengthen thine heart: wait, I say, on the LORD" (Psalm 27:14).

"Commit thy works unto the LORD, and thy thoughts shall be established" (Proverbs 16:3).

God be with you and give you peace—and freedom in Jesus.

CHAPTER
SEVENTEEN

Freedom and Bitterness

"Lest any root of bitterness springing up trouble you, and thereby many be defiled" (Hebrews 12:15).

My friend Herb Kaufman died several years ago. He was a crusty old European who had spent six horrible years serving in the Axis army during World War II. After thc war, he moved to Canada to escape the terrible memories that had accumulated during those years.

But it didn't work out that way. In Canada his marriage broke up, and he became estranged from his two sons. He moved to our little town from Alberta and lived a lonely life. He blamed his wife, his sons, and practically everyone else who crossed his path. He was a hard-shelled man, who seldom dared to open himself to others. When he did open up, he would say, "I'm just a bitter old man!"

And that he was. What about? Everything. You never knew what would set him off. Sometimes, after spewing out bitterness, he would be a little sheepish. But his bitterness was never far from the surface. It ruled his thoughts, his attitudes toward people, and his responses to them. Worst of all was his attitude toward God. And that was how he died.

Bitterness does not just happen to soldiers. It does not happen only to people who had an unusually hard life. It is a problem of humanity. Can you think of any atrocity of the past or present that did not include bitterness of some sort? Such an atrocity happened because people did not deal with the root issues in their lives. They allowed them to fester, and finally they flew into fierce action. In the spring of 2007, a student at Virginia Tech went on a shooting spree, killing some thirty people and wounding others before he killed himself. What was that man trying to communicate by his rampage on that last horrible day of his life? Basically, it was bitterness.

This kind of thing has been going on for a long time. Why else did Cain kill Abel? Why did Joseph's brothers try to get rid of him? Why did the Jews scheme against Jesus? Why do people persecute others today?

Christian believers themselves are not immune to bitterness—even though they might not be as violent about it. The context of our caption verse, Hebrews 12:15, is instruction to believers. We are given a sober warning to be diligent lest we fall into the subtle trap of bitterness that Satan uses to deceive and spoil Christians.

How does it happen? What is bitterness? Bitterness is the heart's response to the things that happen to us and around us. It comes when a hurt makes us sour and cynical—not about one issue alone but about all of life. The attitudes become as bitter and distorted as a mouthful of vinegar. They create emotional bondage that takes away the freedom of peace and joy in our hearts. If not dealt with, bitter attitudes become more and more destructive.

Bitter feelings start out small, just as roots do. But as they grow, they become more deadly. At first, they are hard to detect. But like odorless and tasteless poison in the fountain or the well, they still have deadly effects. The caption verse tells us that if bitterness springs up, it will trouble us, and many will be defiled. That is why the verse begins with "Looking diligently lest any man fail of the grace of God." We want to diligently look for the threads of the roots in our own hearts lest they destroy our peace and rob us of our freedom.

The Devastation of Bitterness

For a number of years, we had a chickweed problem in our garden. It started in a small patch at the edge of the garden. Even though we fought it, we could never get all the tiny roots. Little by little, year after year, it grew and took over more and more of the garden. Eventually the ground became such a mass of tangled roots that the seeds and plants we planted didn't have a chance. They got choked out. The garden was devastated. We had to start over again.

Bitterness does the same to the human heart. It sours the control center within. It is the "everything is against me and I don't like it" feeling. It is a negative reaction to the way things are—plus all that we imagine them to be.

Bitterness is a cruel master. It harasses the soul with the very things it hates. Instead of letting slights and hurts go, bitterness stores them up and keeps rolling them around in the mind. Bitterness toward other people won't even let us get away from them. Those people go with us all day long in our minds. They are with us when we go to sleep and when we wake up.

Bitterness by its very nature focuses on what is wrong with everything rather than on what is right. It keeps its memory sharp by constantly rehearsing its grievances. It continually rubs the open wound—and it only hurts more.

Bitterness blames everything on someone else. "If he would do as he ought, I would not feel the way I do. But since he is the way he is, I am justified in feeling bad toward him." An attitude like that works the same as tightly wrapping a fresh burn; it just drives the heat deeper.

Bitterness devastates relationships because it puts up walls of envy and jealousy. When Joseph's brothers were bitter toward him, they could not speak peaceably with him. And they did not stop until they were rid of him (Genesis 37:4, 28). When King Saul became bitter toward David, "Saul eyed David from that day and forward" (1 Samuel 18:9). It was a downward path for Saul from then on.

Bitterness can invade the home because people live close to each other in daily routines. They know each other's flat sides and faults. Quite likely, each one has desires, preferences, and goals that are important to him. When those desires and dreams are interfered with or dashed, one tends to feel bad toward those who seemingly are responsible for keeping the right things from happening.

God is well aware of the pain that bitterness can inflict on a marriage relationship. He spoke to the matter very directly in Colossians 3:19. "Husbands, love your wives, and be not bitter against them." Why did God single out this particular truth? Is it because bitterness is a special problem that husbands must deal with? Are men likely to blame their wives when things go wrong or against their wishes?

In any case, bitterness is contagious. Hebrews 12 warns us that many can be defiled by a bitter root springing up. That's because people seldom keep bitterness to themselves. It oozes out of them in direct and indirect ways. They spread the seeds of their own problems whenever they have an opportunity. They go fishing for sympathy and try to get support against the persons they do not like. When one bitter heart meets another bitter heart, they usually do not help each other.

The worst devastation that takes place in the heart is bitterness toward God. It is amazing how people take it out on God for what He did not do. One woman announced that she was through with God because of what happened to her. "Did God cause your problem?" she was asked. "Well, no." "Then who did?" "It was the devil!" "Why then are you bitter toward God?" Good question. People make this mistake every day. They blame God for what His enemy has done.

When people are bitter toward God, they keep God from helping them. They are slapping at His outstretched hand. Bitterness brings people to a dark, lonesome place because it takes them away from Him.

After the warning about bitterness, the next verses in Hebrews 12 show us how it worked with a man who went down that road. "Lest there be any fornicator, or profane person, as Esau, who for one morsel of meat sold his birthright. For ye know how that afterward, when he would have inherited the blessing, he was rejected: for he found no place of repentance, though he sought it carefully with tears."

According to Genesis 27, when Esau could not have the blessing he desired, "he cried with a great and exceeding bitter cry." His response showed bitterness, not repentance. His remorse was self-pity and anger. Esau's determination to get even with his brother was so strong that his father sent Jacob away.

We must beware that we are not devastated by bitterness. If we respond bitterly to bad situations, we will be in emotional bondage. We must guard the "fountain" of our lives lest it be contaminated. That is why Proverbs 4:23 instructs us, "Keep thy heart with all diligence; for out of it are the issues of life."

Let's check more closely for the roots of bitterness. Let's ask the Lord to show us our own hearts.

The Roots of Bitterness

Bitterness comes from not making peace with the things that God has allowed in our lives. Instead of accepting them, we let them run around and around in our minds, fanning the flames higher and higher.

Where does it start? The cause may be hard to pinpoint. Several young men from the Middle East were involved in riots and public disturbances. When they were asked what was driving them, they replied, "We were angry." "Angry about what?" "We don't know; we were just angry."

We need to be more specific than that if we hope to stay free from bitterness. We need to look for the roots that produce the fruit.

In many cases, bitterness is suppressed anger. Rather than letting loose in a strong outburst, people allow their anger to seethe and smolder inside them. However, what is going on inside of us rarely stays there. Internal pain can be deadly. It does what it did to a woman a policeman told me about recently. She survived a vehicle crash and looked all right, but she died later because of internal injuries from a misplaced seat belt.

People likely never intend to let their anger become destructive. They might like to think that the old things were put behind, but somehow they don't go away. Instead, they get stewed over. And then something sets them off.

One evening this spring, a friend of ours lit a fire to burn dead grass around his buildings. The fire flashed through the grass, and soon died down. Then the man went to bed. What he did not know was that the fire had crept into a log right beside his hay barn. The next afternoon, many hours later, while he was away, the fire sprang up, roared through the barn, and destroyed it.

We had the same problem one dry summer when we were clearing land. We burned the piles of brush and were satisfied that the fires were out. However, days later, when it was hot and windy, the fire re-emerged. It had gone underground and was smoldering in the roots. With the right circumstances, the fire burst out again.

That is what anger-driven bitterness will do. It may seem to be under control, but then something triggers those suppressed feelings and fuels a blowup that may have seemed unthinkable.

Bitterness is a form of veiled hatred. The lack of generosity toward others often reveals that the veil is very thin. Quite likely, other people see through it more quickly than the bitter person does.

Bitterness may also take the form of a desire for revenge—maybe not in full measure. But the desire is lurking to hurt someone back because of how he hurt us. Subconsciously we watch for the opportunity to retaliate. We want to let him know that he hurt us, and we hope it hurts him to know it. And we enjoy any kind of hardship he might encounter.

Refusing to forgive creates a seedbed for bitterness. We can cling hard to the memory of a wrong that someone did to us. Listen to a bitter person, and you are sure to hear criticisms and accusations against others. You might get the impression that an incident happened two days ago, but then discover that it was years ago. Many a person has discovered that his problem of bitterness was his failure to let go of wrongs. Then they became like poison.

Feeling deprived can generate bitterness. This often comes by comparing what others have with what we don't have. Some people resent that they were deprived of the education they were entitled to. Some resent their age. One healthy-looking man was asked how old he was. His answer: "Eighty-two. Isn't that terrible?" Many people his age would have been happy to be as healthy as he.

Some feel deprived by their social status. They say they are looked down on in the community. One man blamed his nationality because he couldn't seem to keep a job. He said, "It's because I am ———." But his employers said the real problem was his performance.

Some resent that they did not have the economic opportunities others had. The success of others bothers them. They say that the successful ones were born with silver spoons in their mouths. Often they criticize the way people get their money or how they use their money. To them it is never quite right.

Bitterness comes because of not being satisfied with how things are. It comes by comparing themselves with others and not liking what they see. When we begrudge others the advantages they have, it is hard to appreciate anything good about them. Bitterness puts the magnifying glass on them and gives no mercy.

Jealousy and envy foment bitterness. The mother who is on twenty-four-hour duty, the father who works long and hard to provide for his family, or the youth who is needed at home can feel trapped by duty. When viewed from that perspective, the road ahead looks long and dreary.

Bitterness can also show up in the line of Christian duty. We may do what God has called us to do, but in our hearts begrudge the sacrifice it takes. Even our location can trouble us. God does not call everyone to faraway, glamorous-sounding places. He calls some to places where they can pursue life much as before. He lets some people stay in their secure, familiar surroundings and live for Him there. And He calls some to places where much difficulty, sacrifice, and suffering are the norm.

Strangely, at any of these places or levels, each can look over the fence and think that the other has what he would like. Any one of these can quarrel with God about where he is. If that festers, it will cause a kind of bitterness that makes him miserable and useless.

The happenings of life can cause bitterness. Things happen that should not have happened—things that no one can help or change. Accidents, sickness, and suffering—or death itself—can become pits of self-pity and bitterness. If they are not accepted as part of life, bitterness will result.

One man spent much of his life in bitterness because his young son had died. He rejected God because he believed that God had rejected him by allowing his son to die. Other people do the same about much smaller things.

The path to festering bitterness can often be traced. Those who are self-willed and have not learned to give in throughout life are more likely to be bitter. But those who have learned to give up their own way can more readily accept the undesirable things that come into their lives.

A major cause of bitterness is self—unyielded, unbroken, stubborn self. Self wants its own way. It does not like to be told what to do. If it can't have its way, it resists and fights anything that gets in its way. It will lash out at others; it will resist and resent those who get in its way. Hardly anyone can do anything right. If bitter people stood back and looked at themselves, they would realize that they are so miserable they can hardly live with themselves.

We must find answers to these roots of bitterness, because they cloud our relationship with God, destroy our freedom in Him, and make us vulnerable to our own sinful nature. We need help!

Helps for Bitterness

Bitterness is a master at making excuses—especially at shifting the blame. Bitterness tries to make itself comfortable as it is. But is that good enough for God? Is there deliverance from bitterness? Does God have a better way?

First we want to take direction from the Bible. In Ephesians 4:31, among numerous directions for the believer, God tells us, "Let all bitterness, and wrath, and anger, and clamour, and evil speaking, be put away from you, with all malice."

Bitterness must be put away. How can we do that? Bitterness is part of the old nature, or "old man," as he is called in verse 22. Note what must be done: "That ye put off concerning the former conversation the old man, which is corrupt according to the deceitful lusts" (Ephesians 4:22).

How can such a stubborn, selfish part of us be dealt with? The answer is in the next two verses: "Be renewed in the spirit of your mind; and that ye put on the new man, which after God is created in righteousness and true holiness."

Freedom from bitterness is possible only by the power and presence of God in our hearts. The power of the flesh with all its bitterness can only be broken by true repentance for sin and by faith in the Lord Jesus Christ.

Bitter persons must forgive. Much bitterness lives and dwells on what others have done—real or imagined. To be delivered from bitterness, the bitter person must forgive all the people he holds things against. He must resign the right to hold anything against anyone!

That is what Jesus meant when He taught us to pray, "Forgive us our debts, as we forgive our debtors. . . . For if ye forgive men their trespasses, your heavenly Father will also forgive you: but if ye forgive not men their trespasses, neither will your Father forgive your trespasses" (Matthew 6:12–15).

Thanks be to God, when we repent sincerely of our sins, God then gives us the power to forgive others also. He shows us how much more we have violated against Him than what anyone has ever done to us. On the other hand, Jesus gave a stiff sentence if we refuse to forgive: "So likewise shall my heavenly Father do also unto you, if ye from your hearts forgive not every one his brother their trespasses" (Matthew 18:35).

We must surrender. We must give up to God our so-called rights and the demands of our sinful nature. We must admit that when we are bitter, carnal feelings have taken control. Scriptures like Romans 14:17–19 make this clear: "For the kingdom of God is not meat and drink; but righteousness, and peace, and joy in the Holy Ghost. . . . Let us therefore follow after the things which make for peace, and things wherewith one may edify another."

Surrender means yielding to God's will. We accept the need to forgive. We accept the duties of life. We accept the happenings of life as being allowed by God. Even the inequities of life and those things which seem unfair need to be yielded to Him. Jesus gave the perfect example of this when He was in the shadow of the cross. He said, "Not my will, but thine, be done."

Freedom does not require that everything be just right before we can be free. Freedom comes by letting go in our hearts and yielding to God.

Freedom in our hearts comes by trusting God. Without trusting in His goodness, His love, His power, and His involvement in our lives, we find no freedom.

Note what trust did for the psalmist, in Psalm 27:13, 14: "I had fainted, unless I had believed to see the goodness of the LORD in the land of the living. Wait on the LORD: be of good courage, and he shall strengthen thine heart: wait, I say, on the LORD."

Trusting in the goodness of God will sustain us when we are disappointed and distressed. Knowing that God has only good in mind for us strengthens us to wait and to be of good courage.

Another part of this is to trust God in the everyday things of life. Here is what He tells us in Romans 8:28: "And we know that all things work together for good to them that love God, to them who are the called according to his purpose."

One man asked, "What if I fall asleep on the way home, hit a tree, and my wife is killed? Would that be good?" People ask the same question in many other ways.

The answer does not lie in making God responsible for the tragedies that happen. We know He allows them to happen, because obviously there are many ways He could have prevented them. When a friend drowned, we were comforted by the realization that God could have prevented our friend from being there in a hundred different ways.

The satisfying answer to the question above is that God, because of who He is, can make good come out of every happening. Sometimes it may seem impossible, but time has proved that some good does indeed come out of some very difficult circumstances—that is, if they are accepted.

There is freedom in trusting in God's love. Or better yet, we are free to love! "Because the love of God is shed abroad in our hearts by the Holy Ghost which is given unto us" (Romans 5:5), we are called (and enabled) to love others as we want God to love us.

When bitterness is displaced by the love of the Son, we can be free indeed!

Chapter
Eighteen

Freedom and Attitudes Toward Self

"The heart is deceitful above all things, and desperately wicked: who can know it?" (Jeremiah 17:9).

Who is your worst enemy? Does it seem strange to say that you are your own worst enemy and I am mine? Who, if anyone, keeps you from having freedom in your heart? It is not your landlord, or your boss, or your parents, or your spouse, or some other difficult person in your life. It is you!

That should not come as a surprise. By nature, our hearts really work against themselves in the search for freedom. Human nature constantly digs a hole for itself, trying to break through to freedom at the bottom! One of the greatest paradoxes of life is that when the flesh has its own way, it always brings the soul into bondage. So, for the soul to be free, it must be free from the clutches and power of the fleshly nature.

In this chapter we will discuss four common problems that bring the soul into bondage. These problems are as old as the Fall of our first parents. Nowadays we hear supposedly new but deceptive, humanistic answers to these problems—answers that only make the bondage deeper. The problems we want to consider are self-esteem, self-love, self-hatred, and self-pity.

The Problems of the 'Self' Attitudes

Self-esteem says you must have a good opinion of yourself. You must tell yourself how good you are, believe it, and act upon it; and you will get good results.

"How dare she treat me like that!" Frieda fumed. "She suggested I didn't know enough to take charge of the project. She doesn't realize that I just finished that self-help course and learned that I needed to exert myself to my full capacity. I won't take putdowns like that anymore!"

It is true that some people consider themselves worth less than they are. They feel like dirt; and when they act accordingly, they dig the hole of their low self-esteem deeper. Those individuals need to understand what they are worth to God. Certainly they are worth a great deal! Matthew 16:26 asks the question, "What is a man profited, if he shall gain the whole world, and lose his own soul? or what shall a man give in exchange for his soul?" This indicates that our own soul is worth more than the whole world. What God has invested in us at Calvary confirms this truth.

The problem comes when we are concerned that others recognize what we are worth. That becomes self-conceit! People blow themselves up—a little like a puffer fish, which can triple its size to give itself a more massive appearance.

When people pump themselves up to feel better about themselves, they are always in danger that something will puncture their impression of themselves. They must always be on the alert that no one takes advantage of them. It takes high maintenance to protect the thin skin of their image.

It is impossible to be free when one has to be so self-protective, so jealously guarding one's own turf. It is bondage to never be able to be oneself, but to always put on airs.

Self-love promoters say we must love ourselves as we are to love our neighbors. They get this teaching from Matthew 22:39. Notice what Jesus said: "Thou shalt love the Lord thy God with all thy heart, and with all thy soul, and with all thy mind. This is the first and great commandment. And the second is like unto it, Thou shalt love thy neighbour as thyself." They interpret it like this:

"I've been saving my money a long time for this excursion, and nothing will stop me," Leo said flatly. "I'm entitled to this, and I am going to go even if you think I should go help in the hurricane cleanup instead. I worked hard for two years, and it is high time to give myself a treat."

That kind of self-love thinks only about its own well-being, happiness, and benefit. Everything surrounds number one. Self-love is so obsessive and self-serving that there is no room for anything else.

The promoters of self-love say it is the eleventh of the Ten Commandments. After all, the Bible says we are to love our neighbors as ourselves! They seem to think they are the first persons to think of that, and they wonder why it was not emphasized in earlier years. They use this teaching as a good excuse to pamper themselves.

Why does the Bible not emphasize loving ourselves? We don't need to look very far for that answer. It is right within us! "No man ever yet hated his own flesh" (Ephesians 5:29). Most of us do not need to be encouraged to look after our own bodies. Instead, we have to resist self-love from day one.

John 12:25 also helps us to understand what Jesus was talking about. "He that loveth his [self] life shall lose it; and he that hateth his [self] life in this world shall keep it unto life eternal." Self-love is destructive, but not loving self selfishly is constructive.

To really understand how selfish and obnoxious self-love is, we may need to look at other people who have the problem. For we can be so intoxicated with ourselves that we can't see it in ourselves.

Why isn't a person free if he loves himself? Why doesn't that bring supreme satisfaction? It is because our selfish, carnal nature is never satisfied—it never gets enough of itself. It has an insatiable desire that takes it deeper and deeper into slavery to itself. Ask the drug addict or the alcoholic or the free-love advocate when enough is enough. Ask the pleasure lover or the moneymaker.

Self-hatred is the opposite of self-love and is just as damaging. It doesn't like itself or anyone related to itself. "I hate myself and my family. I am ashamed of my last name, and I wish no one knew where I came from. I hide my identity the best I can!" Yvonne said. "I'm not good for anything, and my neighbor just told me I won't ever amount to anything. I wish . . ."

Sometimes it is hard to know whether self-hatred is real or not. People might say very ugly things about themselves in the name of self-hatred. But let someone else say the same thing—and see if they agree with that!

But sometimes a person hates himself as sincerely as he knows how. He doesn't like his family background, he despises his religious background, and he is critical of anything associated with his past. Anything, he thinks, is better than the memories he is stuck with.

Sometimes self-hatred is a person's form of rebellion against what he knows he should be. He turns down help that others try to give him, preferring to think he is hopeless. He does not like where he is, but he claims that the past is to blame for his present predicament.

Religious self-haters feel that the spiritual environment they grew up in did not meet their needs or kept them from finding the answers to life's problems. One religious self-hater repeatedly talked about the religious background he used to have. (I don't know where he thinks his background went.) But blaming his background did seem to make him feel better!

Religious self-haters hate what they were taught. Is it because they don't want to accept the obligations their religious knowledge puts on them? Is it because they don't want to live by it or be judged by it? They try to run away from it—at least in their minds. But that does not set them free. It only wraps them up tighter in themselves.

Another kind of self-hatred comes from failure—constant failure that makes improvement look hopeless. The feeling of guilt rests so heavy and the way out seems so remote that when the sufferer looks inward, he sees little hope—only a very dark picture.

We can never escape something by hating it. If we hate, the problem is only driven deeper.

Self-pity is feeling sorry for oneself. "This is what always happens to me," wailed Woodrow. "I always get the worst of the positions when the group reorganizes. It doesn't help to even be there and to try. I'm just going to sit back and see if anyone notices."

Self-pity says, "I hate it when people say, 'I know how you feel.' Nobody knows how I feel. You can't understand unless you've been where I am, and nobody ever was."

Self-pity has the idea that we have certain rights we are entitled to. It focuses on the modern emphasis of human rights. But it fails to see all the YIELD signs and makes life troublesome for itself and everyone else.

Self-pity takes any problem, regardless of its size, and uses it as an opportunity to throw its shroud over the soul and hold it there. Self-pity has never gotten anyone anywhere but deeper into the very thing it is pitying itself about! And it will keep the way of escape blocked as long as it continues to bewail its condition rather than looking for an escape.

Is there an answer to all the problems that self afflicts itself with? Can we ever hope to be free, with such a selfish, subtle self to deal with?

Finding Answers to the "Self" Problems

What does the Bible say about the flesh or carnal nature?

Let's go back to our caption verse. Jeremiah said that the heart (self) is deceitful and desperately wicked. Self is a survivor. It never gives up trying to get its own way. Just because it may not seem to be exerting itself at the moment does not mean it has given up. Given an opportunity, it will seize control again. Don't be deceived by its deceitfulness!

In Matthew 16:25, Jesus used the term *life,* which means the self-life. "For whosoever will save his life shall lose it: and whosoever will lose his life for my sake shall find it." If we try to keep the self-life, we can't keep it anyway. But if we give it up, we will find real life—the "free indeed" life!

God spoke through Paul in another way, in Galatians 2:20: "I am crucified with Christ: nevertheless I live; yet not I, but Christ liveth in me: and the life which I now live in the flesh I live by the faith of the Son of God, who loved me, and gave himself for me." Paul said he was crucified with Christ. What did he mean? "Crucified with" means "to be joined to another by impaling on a cross." He said that his personal self-life was joined to the dying Christ on the cross in death to self, and that he then lived the "Christ in me" life.

Is the self-life then dead—buried and gone forever—as some teach? We wish! But that is not how it is. The Bible tells us, in Romans 6:6, "Knowing this, that our old man [flesh, self-life] is crucified with him." How does this work? See verse 11: "Likewise *reckon* ye also yourselves to be dead indeed unto sin, but alive unto God through Jesus Christ our Lord."

To reckon means "to consider, estimate, and treat as." We are to treat the self part of us as dead. We are not to feed it or pamper it, but keep it in forced, solitary confinement just as if it were a dethroned despot. If fed or given an opportunity, it will sneak forth and take control again.

Galatians 5:17 gives us another insight: "For the flesh lusteth against [opposes] the Spirit, and the Spirit against the flesh: and these are contrary the one to the other: so that ye cannot do the things that ye would." The battle is on! God wants the Spirit to keep us free, and Satan wants to take us captive. Read on in Galatians 5 to see the results, depending on whom we choose to let reign in our lives.

All this adds up to the fact that God has made power available so that self does not need to ruin our freedom and joy. Obviously, self dare not reign in our control tower. Its insistent desires must be denied. Instead, God's way must be the law of our lives.

Now let's retrace our steps through self-esteem, self-love, self-hatred, and self-pity to see what lessons we can learn and what answers may be found.

Self-esteem must die so that Christ can live in us. The self that wants to be exalted instead of Christ must be denied, put down, and crucified. Self wants the throne of our hearts—the throne Jesus Christ will not share with any other. It can't be both.

God tells us how we are to feel about ourselves, in Romans 12:3: "For I say, through the grace given unto me, to every man that is among you, not to think of himself more highly than he ought to think; but to think soberly, according as God hath dealt to every man the measure of faith."

Actually, God places a high value on the human race, or He would not have given the best heaven had in order to provide forgiveness and redemption for the human race. As sons and daughters of the Most High, we indeed are precious to Him—not of ourselves but because of Him! We have nothing to glory in of ourselves. "But God forbid that I should glory, save in the cross of our Lord Jesus Christ, by whom the world is crucified unto me, and I unto the world" (Galatians 6:14).

Self-love must be replaced with love for God. We must love Him for who He is. We must love what He loves and hate what He hates. His wishes become our commands. Then, and only then, can we be delivered from the tyranny of our selfish carnal nature. Loving God sets us free from ourselves to be truly His.

Self-hatred must be replaced by hating what God hates. This is possible only by accepting God's loving view of the value of humanity. Realizing He loves us and wants to restore us ought to melt our self-rejecting hearts with appreciation and acceptance of His provisions for us. When His love fills our hearts, we understand that He has a plan and purpose for each of us.

Freedom comes when we hate what God hates and love what He loves!

Self-pity is changed to freedom only by letting go of our supposed rights. We must look through the clouds for what God wants for us. We must be tuned to God's plan and desire rather than our own. When we ask for nothing but God's will, self is forgotten.

Finally, freedom comes from living for the Lord instead of for self. It comes by loving His cause and kingdom on the earth and being loyal to it. We must allow Jesus Christ to be enthroned in our hearts and to be honored in all of life. When self raises its ugly, selfish head within us, we must put it down by the authority and power of God in our hearts.

Faith in God, trusting Him to work His will in our lives through Jesus Christ, is the only way to have true freedom.

"If the Son therefore shall make you free, ye shall be free indeed."

Chapter
Nineteen

Freedom by Self-denial and Cross Bearing

"If any man will come after me, let him deny himself, and take up his cross, and follow me" (Matthew 16:24).

The previous chapter was about "self" matters. The four we looked at are enemies of our freedom and have to be dealt with to have victory. Now we come to a good kind of "self" that brings freedom to our hearts. It sets us free from the other "selves" and encourages us to live for the Lord.

Self-denial is both negative and positive. It is both painful and powerful. It hurts one part of us but helps another. It takes us from bondage to freedom.

Ralph rubbed his head. His thoughts marched round and round through his mind. He felt convicted of wrongdoing. But he liked his new, short, stylish haircut because of how manageable it was—at least that was what he was telling himself. He knew that his church said that following the hair fads was born out of a desire to fit into the social culture. Ruefully, he also remembered that not so many years ago, he had argued for the need to wear his hair long—because of how manageable *that* was. Which way was it? What was driving him?

Was Brother Luke right? He had suggested it might be a "self" problem—self-will. Self-will? Why would it be that? What were the evidences of that? He squirmed. He had to admit that his reasons in both cases were flimsy and affected by the times. "But," he argued with himself, "why should my church care about such things?" And, in all honesty, he would need to admit there were other matters just like this that cut across his grain—matters of his own that the church had no business bothering him about.

After weeks of struggle, Ralph came to the point where he acknowledged to himself that it was indeed his self-life that was driving him. He realized too that his church was trying to help him on the heavenward way. Beyond that, he saw that the issue between him and the church was really an issue between him and God. He saw that he was forced to choose between the two—his will or God's will. Self had to go, or God would go.

Ralph fell to his knees. He laid it all out before the Lord. He surrendered his self-will. He cried for mercy, pardon, and the power to truly deny himself. The Lord answered with peace. His heart was flooded with a new freedom. "I must tell Brother Luke it works!"

That is the good news: self can be dealt with. No one has to be a slave to it if he takes the way of self-denial and cross bearing.

What Are Self-denial and Cross Bearing?

Let's start with denial. To deny is to say no. When someone denies a request we make to him, he says no. It also means to disown, to have no connection with. Peter did that when he denied Jesus. "But he [Peter] began to curse and to swear, saying, I know not this man of whom ye speak" (Mark 14:71).

Now then, how are we to deny the self in us that calls itself number one? Self must be put down. To deal with self, we must die to self. Self is no longer glorified. Personal reputation is not supreme. When we say no to self, we treat this self like a stranger whom we have rejected and put out of our lives. It has no right to insist on anything for itself.

Suppose an employer said to another employer's worker, "Come help me today. I want you." What would a loyal employee say to such a demand? He would say, "I can't; I'm already employed."

God expects us to say the same thing to the old life. He states this clearly in Romans 6:6. "Knowing this, that our old man [self life] is crucified with him, that the body of sin might be destroyed, that henceforth we should not serve sin."

Let's move on to cross bearing. What is that? Jesus said that everyone who followed Him would have his own cross to bear. He meant that following Him would often be painful and inconvenient, as if one were carrying a literal cross everywhere he went. He meant also that cross bearing ends only one way—in death to the cross bearer. The only life one has ever known must be left behind. A new "self" can only come to life after the old self has died.

Obviously, self-denial and cross bearing rise and fall together. They demand a full dedication of the whole person to God.

Why Self-denial and Cross Bearing Bring Freedom

Both God and Satan promise freedom to their followers. Here is what the Bible tells us about Satan's offer: "While they promise them liberty, they themselves are the servants of corruption: for of whom a man is overcome, of the same is he brought in bondage" (2 Peter 2:19). That is the same liberty Satan promised Eve in the Garden.

In spite of all the fulfillment that self and sin promise, they bring slavery. The flesh takes control and ruins itself.

Self and sin wrap the soul in a small, selfish world. The spirit starves because the flesh is being fed.

But here is God's side. He gives us "exceeding great and precious promises: that by these ye might be partakers of the divine nature, having escaped the corruption that is in the world through lust" (2 Peter 1:4). After listing the steps of the new life, He promises, "For so an entrance shall be ministered unto you abundantly into the everlasting kingdom of our Lord and Saviour Jesus Christ" (2 Peter 1:11).

What a contrast between Satan's promises and the Lord's! Satan promises gratification now and tries to hide the fact of eternal woe (not to mention a multitude of woes between now and eternity). The Lord does not promise ease and luxury now but points to the future satisfaction of escaping corruption and entering heaven (and quite a few satisfactions between now and then).

When we deny our flesh and accept the cross, we have freedom from the flesh. No longer will we allow it to have its debauching way. Instead of that, the Holy Spirit breathes His heavenly power and life into us. We are freed from one and free to live in the other!

This involves much more than a cold, calculated choice. It has to do with love. Jesus said we will love one or the other of two masters. We read also, "If any man love the world, the love of the Father is not in him" (1 John 2:15). Thankfully, the reverse is also true. "He that dwelleth in love dwelleth in God, and God in him" (1 John 4:16).

If we love God and dwell in Him, we are dwelling in the light. That gives us marvelous privileges. As 1 John 1:7 puts it, "If we walk in the light, as he is in the light, we have fellowship one with another, and the blood of Jesus Christ his Son cleanseth us from all sin."

These things can only happen as we are willing to deny self and bear the cross of discipleship to our Lord Jesus Christ.

Naturally, none of this makes sense until you see it and experience it. The flesh blinds the spirit to such possibilities of freedom because it does not want to be bound. Neither does it realize how God changes the mind and heart about sin and selfishness.

Once you enter into the new life, then the old life no longer makes sense. People who experience the change look back and wonder how they could have been so blind and self-destructive. Even if they lived morally upright lives, they lacked the prospect of the future life that God has for His own.

Once you have new life, you want to keep it. How can that be done?

Staying Free

First, remember that the flesh is never completely destroyed. It is never satisfied, and it never gives up wanting its way. Its cries for fulfillment come in the form of various temptations. If we yield to them, we lose our freedom and are in bondage again.

Our emotions feel the pressure of the conflict. If we allow something to whet the appetite of our flesh, the battle rages within between the flesh and the Spirit. If we yield to the flesh, we know what follows—guilt. And our peace of heart and mind is gone.

To stay free, we need to stay within a safety zone. We have coyotes in our area. They usually stay out of sight, but they try to lure our dogs away after them. If they get the dogs far enough away from the safety of home, they attack them. Other predators do the same. They always attack the animals who wander away from the flock first. If we loiter in the areas where sin abounds, we are asking for trouble. The only way to stay free is to keep saying no to the flesh—day after day, whenever the call of the flesh comes.

This is possible only by the power of the Holy Spirit within. The Christ-in-us life gives satisfaction. And when we live life seriously, the appeals of sin and the flesh lose their grip and can be seen for what they really are. The Holy Spirit will show us the pain and price that yielding to sin brings. He will prod our consciences when we are on dangerous ground, and remind us to take steps to escape.

When we deny self, bear the cross, and follow Christ willingly, our spirits can be free because "where the Spirit of the Lord is, there is liberty" (2 Corinthians 3:17). Surely, there is nothing better than being at peace with God through the Lord Jesus Christ.

Chapter
Twenty

Freedom and Worry

"Take therefore no thought for the morrow: for the morrow shall take thought for the things of itself" (Matthew 6:34).

Worry is not a pleasant companion. Its undue anxiety eats away at the soul. It occupies the mind and robs it of peace and joy and confidence. It works against freedom in the heart.

This does not mean there is nothing in life to be deeply concerned about. It does not mean there are no cares in life. It does not mean there will never be things that give us heavy hearts. That comes with life.

This chapter does not try to minimize those realities and struggles of life. But it is about helping us to not be caught in distracting care. It is about relating properly to the concerns and burdens we have in life so as not to be caught in the net of undue anxiety. Since dealing with worry is a necessary part of being free indeed, we will talk about life from that side.

You have met people who are ruled by worry. They seem to thrive on the what-ifs of life. They can hardly enjoy a beautiful day, because it might rain. Even when their health is good, they wonder what ailment might be incubating inside them. They look at world events with trepidation. They worry about the future, their children, and their grandchildren.

One might say, "Don't they have a point? Might the worriers be right?" Yes, they might be. And the things they worry about do happen sometimes. And they happen to people who don't worry as well! If our child does not come home when we expected, and the ambulance goes past our house, we'll think about it.

The whole point about worry is the way we look at life and respond to it. Instead of seeing life through the eye of faith, worry looks at it through the eye of fear and aloneness. Worry is one thing Jesus was addressing when He said, "Take therefore no thought for the morrow: for the morrow shall take thought for the things of itself. Sufficient unto the day is the evil thereof" (Matthew 6:34).

What Is Worry?

Worry is runaway dread of what might happen. Worry and imagination are close partners because they both feed on the fear of what *might* happen. Waiting for test results from the hospital lab gives ample time to imagine what they might show. After all, wasn't that how Aunt Ada first found out about her terminal disease? The imagination can run wild.

Worry produces vivid, true-to-life images. The mind turns its fear over and over until it becomes real. Worry conjures up worst-case scenarios that rush through the mind with strong authority and haunting impressions. Job knew what it was like. "For the thing which I greatly feared is come upon me, and that which I was afraid of is come unto me" (Job 3:25).

Worry specializes on the future, because you cannot worry about something that has already happened. You cannot really worry about getting cancer when you already know you have it. As long as it has not happened yet, you have no way of knowing what it will really be like—or if it is there at all. Hence the worry.

Many people have the notion that by worrying they can prepare themselves for trouble. At least they get no nasty surprises that way, since they expect trouble. But no one can keep an airplane from crashing by chewing his nails. No one can keep Grandma from falling off a stepladder in Lancaster County by worrying about it in Holmes County.

A schoolteacher put a sign above his chalkboard which said, "Don't just sit there! Worry!" But that was strictly a joke. Worry in itself accomplishes nothing. Nothing good, anyhow. It is common knowledge that worry causes stomach ulcers. Who knows what all else it might cause!

Why is it so easy to worry?

The Tendency to Worry

We are apt to worry, because life is full of things that are uncontrollable. So many things could happen to us! And sometimes they do happen. In light of what could happen, we feel vulnerable. We know we can't control all the unknowns, for we are not equal to them. We can't choose the time or place these things might come. Life is much bigger than we are.

People worry about their health. Since health cannot be guaranteed or controlled, people at least want assurance of good health care and enough financial security to make sure they can afford the help they might need. More and more, cradle-to-grave health care has become a political issue because people want the government to take responsibility for them.

People worry about their assets. They want them to be secure. But fires, floods, earthquakes, and sickness are no respecters of persons. So people salve their worries with insurance policies. That way, if something does happen, the damage will not overwhelm their economic abilities. The insurance world turns on that axis. They play the what-if tune to the hilt.

So do the fire alarm salesmen (not that I am opposed to fire alarms). After one of our children was born, a salesman showed up at our house. He had pictures of burning homes and vivid descriptions of how people suffered and perished in houses without fire alarms. He pushed all the "worry buttons" he could. He tried to make us feel afraid and very irresponsible even to go to bed that night without his protection devices.

What effect does worry have on us? Why does it become such a prison for our souls? Let's try to understand what it does to our freedom.

The Traps of Worry

Worry paralyzes the readiness to take constructive action. It makes any action seem useless and hopeless against all the fears. It robs us of the ability to see any light at the end of the tunnel without thinking it might be an approaching train!

Worry takes the joy out of living. When the present and the future look dim and threatening, how can the soul be free? When it is impossible to see the good in life and to expect better things, the soul is locked up in a dark dungeon.

Worry saps tremendous energy from the body. Worrying is harder than working. Focusing on things like tragic world events or natural disasters robs the attention from things that might be helpful if tended to.

Worry eclipses faith. It blocks God out and focuses on its own fears and imagination. When faith would place the matter in God's hands, worry refuses to listen. It insists that matters are out of control and beyond retrieving.

There must be a right way to look at life!

Taming Worry

We speak of taming worry because there is a productive side to worry that can be helpful if kept in check. Perhaps a better word for it would be *concern.* It gets us moving. Samuel Johnson once put it this way: "Depend upon it, sir, when a man knows he is to be hanged in a fortnight, it concentrates his mind wonderfully."

Effective planning and action can help tame worry. Instead of worrying about whether we can get somewhere in a certain amount of time, we just need to leave earlier. Instead of wondering if the tires are good enough for wet roads, we can replace them. Instead of worrying whether a check will bounce, we can keep our checkbook balance current. And if we are worried about a house fire, we can provide alarms and fire extinguishers, and plan escape routes.

Analyzing one's worries can help tame worry. One chronic worrier made his own new worry list every two weeks. He was quite amazed to discover that by the time he made a new one, most of the old concerns were gone! He found this to be a consistent pattern.

Later, to become more efficient at worrying, he decided to delegate one hour each evening specifically to worry. During the day, when worries would come up, he found relief by promising himself he would worry about them properly in the evening. At least he had pleasant days!

The next step was to cut the evening worry hour down to half an hour. And he was able to do it. Later he decided to skip some days until eventually he found that life went on quite well without his worry times.

Another man kept record of his worries. He discovered that 40 percent of his worries were about things that would never happen. Thirty percent of them were about past decisions he could not change. Twelve percent were about other people's criticism of him. Ten percent were about his health. He concluded that the other 8 percent were legitimate. He could now disregard the majority of his worries and concentrate on the ones that mattered!

Determining what can't be helped can help relieve worry. A circuit rider often needed to cross an unpredictable river in all kinds of weather. He said he had one fixed rule about that river: "I never cross it until I get there." Treating life that way will put many worries in their proper place!

Considering the promises of God can help tame worry. When we worry, we are listening to our doubts, fears, and imaginations more seriously than to God.

Here is one of God's promises, from Isaiah 43:2: "When thou passest through the waters, I will be with thee; and through the rivers, they shall not overflow thee: when thou walkest through the fire, thou shalt not be burned; neither shall the flame kindle upon thee."

Just before Jesus went back to heaven, He gave His followers a similar promise of support, in Matthew 28:19, 20: "Go ye therefore, and teach all nations, baptizing them in the name of the Father, and of the Son, and of the Holy Ghost: teaching them to observe all things whatsoever I have commanded you: and, lo, I am with you alway, even unto the end of the world. Amen."

Jesus also gave some clear, practical direction about worrying, in Matthew 6. (Note that He used "no thought" when He talked about worry.) "Therefore I say unto you, Take no thought for your life, what ye shall eat, or what ye shall drink; nor yet for your body, what ye shall put on" (verse 25). "Wherefore, if God so clothe the grass of the field, which to day is, and to morrow is cast into the oven, shall he not much more clothe you, O ye of little faith?" (verse 30). "Take therefore no thought for the morrow: for the morrow shall take thought for the things of itself. Sufficient unto the day is the evil thereof" (verse 34).

When we take Jesus' words seriously, it settles a host of worries.

Philippians 4:6–9 provides positive answers for worry. Study this carefully to see how it will help tame worry. "Be careful for nothing; but in every thing by prayer and supplication with thanksgiving let your requests be made known unto God. And the peace of God, which passeth all understanding, shall keep your hearts and minds through Christ Jesus. Finally, brethren, whatsoever things are true, whatsoever things are honest, whatsoever things are just, whatsoever things are pure, whatsoever things are lovely, whatsoever things are of good report; if there be any virtue, and if there be any praise, think on these things. Those things, which ye have both learned, and received, and heard, and seen in me, do: and the God of peace shall be with you."

God gives more direction in 1 Peter 5:7: "Casting all your care upon him; for he careth for you." What more could God have said, and how much more tenderly could He have put it?

It is true that not everything works out as we might have preferred. God's Word admits this: "Many are the afflictions of the righteous." But then it adds, "But the

Lord delivereth him out of them all" (Psalm 34:19). Jesus said, "Ye shall be betrayed both by parents, and brethren, and kinsfolks, and friends; and some of you shall they cause to be put to death. . . But there shall not an hair of your head perish" (Luke 21:16, 18). Isaac Watts said, "Thy saints in all this glorious war / Shall conquer though they die."

Last, taming tension becomes real through a personal relationship with God. We trust in Him because we have confidence in who He is. We believe in Him because of His past record. Has God ever let anyone down? Has He left them forsaken and downtrodden? Not if they looked to Him.

God expects us to do our part. We are to take our responsibility in life seriously and do what we can. But then, once we have done that, we need to leave the rest to Him.

"Thou wilt keep him in perfect peace, whose mind is stayed on thee: because he trusteth in thee. Trust ye in the Lord for ever: for in the Lord JEHOVAH is everlasting strength" (Isaiah 26:3, 4).

That is freedom!

CHAPTER
TWENTY-ONE

Freedom by Forgiving

"And forgive us our debts,
as we forgive our debtors" (Matthew 6:12).

"You'll pay for this!" That is the natural tendency when someone hurts us. At least, we think, the other person should come forward, admit he was guilty, and apologize.

But what if he does nothing of the sort and feels no obligation to do so? We are stuck with the pain, and we have to decide what to do about it. We can let the matter haunt us, taking it with us to bed, to mealtimes, to work, and to recreation. Or we can find answers for the problem.

Marvin and Michael were twins. They shared a bedroom. They played and worked together and had the normal mixture of joys and sorrows, delights and disappointments, misunderstandings and mistakes.

But there was such a difference between the boys! Michael became increasingly critical of his home. He felt he always got the short end of things. Others, especially Marvin, had more advantages and privileges. Invariably, Michael got stuck with the most undesirable chores. His friends in other homes had it much better than he. They had more liberty. They could make decisions for themselves, while he always felt boxed in by his inconsiderate parents.

Finally Michael left home. Now he was free!

But life outside was not what he had thought. Happiness did not come as easily as he had expected. Neither had he left his home behind—especially the bad memories. They were at his fingertips, and at the least opportunity, he shared them freely.

As time went on, Michael was surprised to find many more "unfair" things. His list of difficult people and what they had done to him was growing. Nothing slipped by him. Even his wife had a hard time gaining his approval.

Marvin was the opposite. He was as sweet as Michael was sour. Sure, he had disappointments. He had to deal with the same weaknesses in his boyhood home as Michael did. But they did not stick to him like flypaper. He left home with many happy memories—and made many more!

Sometimes Michael would try to refresh Marvin's memory about how bad things had been. He could tell him exact times and places and just what had happened. Marvin, after sorting through the cobwebs, vaguely remembered. Then he would say, "So what?"

But when Marvin rehearsed happy memories, Michael could hardly remember. If he did remember, he admitted it grudgingly and always followed with "But . . ."

These two brothers demonstrate how life works. We can go through life all loaded up with hurts and wrongs. We can keep detailed records and hold tightly to grudges. Or we can rise up against this kind of bondage and look for another option.

Why Must We Be Forgiving?

Our lives can easily become miserable like Michael's. It is the natural way to respond to the negatives in life. But if we do what seems natural, we will end up with the same outlook on life as Michael's. And who wants that?

Failure to forgive can trouble those who want to make peace. Sometimes when there is a grievance, the offender is ready to do whatever it takes to settle it. However, the unforgiving person is not ready to make peace because he doesn't want to give up his feelings. He prefers to keep his grievances alive and active.

Lack of forgiveness leads to long-term bitterness—a bitterness that lashes out against everything and everyone—home, parents and their values, church friends, perceived enemies. One young man, whose teacher-father spent much time in schoolwork, said he hated his school because it robbed him of his father. But resenting the school made him resent his father too. His resentment robbed him of his father as effectively as his father's work did.

Bitterness leads us to suspect other people's motives. Before they ever do wrong, or even while they are doing undeniable good, we question their motives. "Yes, he's doing the right thing, but for the wrong reason," we say. "He just wants to look good."

Suspicion leaves no margin for error. We hold others to a high standard and despise anything else. Even if others were impeccable in character and performance, we would find something to criticize and to hold against them.

Failure to forgive others will finally lead us to resent God Himself. Since He could have prevented our troubles, everything must be His fault. However, we must let go of this idea in order to have peace with Him. Someone called it "forgiving God." Although God never needs to be forgiven, we may need to consciously put an end to any bitterness toward Him.

This matter of conscious forgiveness needs a word more. Sometimes people sweep resentful memories under the rug but never deal with them. Unfortunately, such memories don't stay under the carpet. They continually surface to sap our spirits. Problems like this can be subtle and hard to pinpoint, but they are real. They throw a dark shadow over a person's soul, while the harbored grudges eat away at the soul.

There is something about forgiveness that we have not touched yet.

The Obligation to Be Forgiving

We are often reminded that we must forgive in order to receive forgiveness from God. Let's think about that.

Jesus taught us to pray, "Forgive us our debts, as we forgive our debtors." Then He added, "For if ye forgive men their trespasses, your heavenly Father will also forgive you: but if ye forgive not men their trespasses, neither will your Father forgive your trespasses" (Matthew 6:12, 14, 15).

After telling the story of a servant who refused to forgive his fellow servant and ended up losing his master's forgiveness, Jesus said, "So likewise shall my heavenly Father do also unto you, if ye from your hearts forgive not every one his brother their trespasses" (Matthew 18:35).

Why is God so emphatic about our forgiving others to have our sins forgiven by Him? What is the connection? Does forgiving others earn us forgiveness? Of course not! We can never do enough good to earn one bit of forgiveness. What then?

Simply this: God knows what happens in people's hearts when they are truly sorry for their sins and come to Him pleading for forgiveness. He knows that when people truly repent, they realize they have sinned against God much more than anyone else in the world could have wronged them. God knows that when people are truly broken before

Him, they will not feel justified in trying to settle issues with others. They will cast themselves at His feet in utter unworthiness for such a gift as forgiveness.

Further, if we do not forgive others, we cannot even understand God's forgiveness.

The servant in Matthew 18, who owed his master millions and millions, demonstrated this. We wonder how a man could be forgiven so much and then go out and wring a fellow servant's neck and throw him into prison for a mere twenty dollars! What was his problem?

Let's go back to the deeply indebted servant's request to his master. He said, "Have patience with me, and I will pay thee all." Of course, the master knew that the servant could not begin to pay, so he dealt with him on that basis. "Then the lord of that servant was moved with compassion, and loosed him, and forgave him the debt." The master tore up the record and canceled the debt—just like that!

But did the servant understand? Did he realize that he was a free man who owed nothing, by a mere stroke of the merciful lord's word? Or was it too good to be true, that he did not fathom its meaning? Was he still thinking, "I will pay thee all"? If he was still in a payment mode, no wonder he was out there to get every dollar he could.

Forgiveness means laying aside both "I must pay God for my sins" and "You must pay me."

How Forgiving Sets Us Free

When one person wrongs another person, it creates an unresolved relationship between the two. The wronged person can become a captive in bitterness and self-pity by holding on to the memory of what the wrongdoer did. The only way for the wronged person to be free is to forgive.

In New Testament times, prisoners were often chained to Roman soldiers. But just as truly, the soldiers were chained to their prisoners. As long as they were chained, the soldiers could not get away from their prisoners any more than their prisoners could get away from them. Once the moment came that a prisoner could go away free, the soldier could walk away free as well. Forgiveness works that way. Once we set another person free, we can go free ourselves.

Of course we still have to answer the question one man put so concisely: "How do I unhook him?" Some people have been terribly abused and violated. They have to deal with painful, haunting memories. How can they lay them all down?

That is a searching question, because Jesus said we must forgive "from [our] hearts" (Matthew 18:35). Forgiveness is not just a "Yes, I'll forgive you, but . . ." We are to forgive as God forgives. And to make that more personal, how do we want God to forgive us?

Furthermore, forgiveness involves realizing that we have no rights of our own. It means giving up the supposed right to feel resentful about what happened. It means that, on our part, no one owes us anything—no apologies, no restitution, nothing.

Obviously, if this is the kind of forgiveness God is looking for—if it must penetrate our whole being, we can never do it by ourselves. Only God's grace can make it possible to forgive like that. Only that grace can soften and mellow our hearts, molding our perception of others and enabling us to forgive.

Practically speaking, forgiveness commits the matter to God and leaves the other person's responsibility between God and him. When Jesus on the cross said, "Father, forgive them," it did not mean that His tormentors could go free from their responsibility before God. It meant that He was leaving the matter between them and God. He "committed himself to him that judgeth righteously" (1 Peter 2:23). Stephen displayed a similar spirit before he was stoned to death.

Job faced a difficult situation. His three "friends" had added anguish upon anguish to his suffering by claiming it was the result of his own wickedness. After God vindicated Job, there was something Job was to do: he must pray for his friends. The result? "And the Lord turned the captivity of Job, when he prayed for his friends" (Job 42:10). Now Job was truly free because he could freely pray for them!

The story of Jacob illustrates the same lesson. Jacob had gotten himself into a tight spot with his brother, Esau, and now the moment of truth had come. During the night before they were to meet, Jacob went through a terrible struggle. According to Genesis 32, he wrestled until dawn with a man who finally touched the hollow of his thigh and put it out of joint. Jacob did not let go until the man blessed him and even changed his name. "Thy name shall be called no more Jacob, but Israel: for as a prince hast thou power with God and with men, and hast prevailed."

Jacob went lame in body, but something was set free inside of him that night. He had turned the whole matter over to God, come what may. And, true to form, God turned the showdown into a reconciliation between the two estranged brothers.

Sometimes we struggle more than we ought. We are too slow to let go. But when we finally put matters into God's hand, He can work in ways that are far beyond our comprehension. He can heal relationships that seemed impossible to mend while we were demanding them to be fixed in our selfish ways. And even if the other party does not allow the relationship to be healed, we can still be free in forgiving freely.

Freedom by forgiving is not a once-and-done matter. It is a condition of the heart that must stay current in our lives on a daily basis. We might think we are forgiving, but then something comes along that triggers painful memories and even some resentment. What can we do? How can we keep our freedom by forgiving?

Staying Free

The pit of an unforgiving spirit is a deep one. If not dealt with by the power of God, it will latch onto even small things and hold the soul captive with suspicion and surmising. The root of bitterness, spoken of in Hebrews 12:15, then emerges, troubling not only us but others as well. Satan is there to use it to his advantage and to our destruction.

The Holy Spirit can help in this. But we must take His direction seriously. The following verses, from Ephesians 4:30–32, make it clear that He is with us to help us do what we cannot do of ourselves.

"Grieve not the holy Spirit of God, whereby ye are sealed unto the day of redemption. Let all bitterness, and wrath, and anger, and clamour, and evil speaking, be put away from you, with all malice: and be ye kind one to another, tenderhearted, forgiving one another, even as God for Christ's sake hath forgiven you."

If we live like that, how much hold can an unforgiving spirit get on us? And if we deal with the root of bitterness or a critical spirit stirring within, how far can it get? However, if we slip away from the directions found in these verses, the Holy Spirit is grieved and cannot do His intended work in our hearts.

Then too, we must keep on rejoicing in the forgiveness God has graciously given to us. We must stay keenly conscious of how much we have been forgiven. If we want to rise above our circumstances, we dare not be bashful about praising the Lord for His mercy and goodness to us!

Things will continue to arise in life that we cannot explain or change. Therefore we must continue to commit ourselves to our loving, sovereign God. What He does with these things is up to Him. He will, in due time and in His own way, rectify all things. Only if we have such a commitment can we escape the bitter bondage of an unforgiving heart.

The Witness of Forgiveness

Forgiving love is powerful. Though baffling to the public, it communicates better than thousands of words. Think of the time when an intruder shot ten students in a one-room Amish school in eastern Pennsylvania. Someone observed that the willingness of the victims' families to forgive the killer jolted the world as much as the incident itself.

When the barriers in our hearts are replaced with love, it shows. We are not only able to be nice to people; we can genuinely love them without holding anything against them. God wants to use such expressions of love to reveal His true nature to all men and to mellow the hearts of others.

When we have forgiving hearts, we can sympathize with the struggles of others. When we remember the desolation of our own hearts and how much we need to be forgiven, we can truly pity others. Our attitude frees us to reach out to them in Christian love. We can even hope that God deals with them as mercifully as He has dealt with us!

God does not want His light to be hidden under a bushel. He uses His people's forgiveness to show the world His heart in a way that little else can. "Let your light so shine before men, that they may see your good works, and glorify your Father which is in heaven" (Matthew 5:16).

"Forgive, and ye shall be forgiven" (Luke 6:37). Forgive, and ye shall be free!

CHAPTER
TWENTY-TWO

Freedom and Rejection

Have you ever felt rejected? It is a lonely, hurt feeling, isn't it. It can rob us of the freedom of joy and happiness if we allow it to. Here is how it can go.

Norma heard that their school was adding another classroom and would need another teacher. Her heart leaped! She had always dreamed of being a teacher and had even substituted several times. Day after day shc waited, hoping she would be asked. But nothing happened. No word. Then she heard that her friend had been asked to teach. Norma was crushed.

Richard heard his father talking with his uncle about filling the silo. He heard his father say, "So you're going to have to find more help?" Richard's eyes lit up. Maybe he would be asked. How he enjoyed running machinery! But that evening he learned that another cousin had been asked.

Benjamin went eagerly to the brethren's meeting at his church. He was enthused about helping to clean up tornado damage in the next county. He had already talked to several others about their going with him. At church his idea was well received, and a leader for the project was chosen. But—that leader was someone else.

Several women were discussing what to bring for the fellowship meal next Sunday. Melinda contributed a few ideas. But after the meal was planned, Melinda went home and told her husband, "No one heard me."

If we think about it, this kind of thing has happened to all of us. And if we think about it too much, it will seem worse and worse because we see it more and more. We will make ourselves ever more miserable and less worthy of any opportunities that do come our way.

Why are we sensitive to these things? Partly because we somehow attach our self-worth to them. The more recognition we get, the more valuable we feel. The more rejection we face (or what we perceive as rejection), the less valuable we feel. We assume other people feel the same way about us. The more sensitive we become, the smaller the box we make for ourselves to live in.

There is such a thing as genuine rejection, and we will address it later in the chapter. At this point we are dealing with the kind of problem that seems big to us, but may or may not really be so.

Possible Responses

When we are overlooked and things don't go our way, we can do like the boy on the playground who gathers his glove and bat and goes home. His actions say, "If I can't have my way, I won't play."

If my opinion doesn't carry, I can feel put down. I can take it personally and go away nursing hurt feelings. I can figure out who got his way during the discussion, and then think back over the months or even years and say, "This has been going on for a long time."

We can say, "Since they don't need me more than that, I'll go do something else. The next time I'll stay off the ballot altogether. I can't handle being put down like that again."

When these things happen, we can call ourselves mistreated. Why do people treat me like this? Don't they have any concern for how I feel? Don't they know how it feels to be put down like this?

Perhaps we feel mistrusted. Why am I passed by when others are chosen? Is it because they don't trust me? Is it my family name? Is it because my brother did not do well when he was asked? Is it because I don't have the same background as most of them do? There is nothing more painful and discouraging than not being trusted. What shall I do?

We can call it being misunderstood. Why don't people understand that I really enjoy leading out in projects? Don't they remember how well I did at organizing the other time? Don't they realize that I would have done much better than the one they asked?

These are all destructive responses that are not new to our nature. But such responses make us uncomfortable, even while they seem justified. Besides, such responses make it all the more likely that what we call "rejection" will happen again—and again. Why? Because negative responses bring negative results. The Bible tells us how one man handled his rejection.

Ahithophel took this attitude to an extreme. He gave advice to Absalom—good advice. (It was too good for a bad man like Absalom, and God made sure it was not used.) Although we may not know what all drove Ahithophel, when his advice was rejected in favor of another man's, he went out and hanged himself. What a terrible, destructive response! And though people may not hang themselves physically, some may hang themselves emotionally over such things.

Let's think about what happens when we respond negatively.

Practical Results

We need to ask ourselves, "Where do such negative responses take us?" Isn't it true that they take us away from where we want to be?

We want to be happy, but counting up our rejection slips will make us unhappy. We want to be sensible, but we get pretty far away from that if we let our imaginations take over, blaming our rejection on things people never even thought of. We want to have friends, but nursing our sense of rejection can easily make us standoffish and as prickly as a porcupine. We become critical observers rather than a part of what is happening.

We don't want to be thought of as difficult persons, but we can make ourselves difficult indeed. Others may see that something got into us, but they may not have any idea what it is. They might keep their distance even more—not because they want to, but because they don't know what went wrong.

If we are too sensitive to rejection, people might avoid getting close to us. If they always have to walk on eggshells and be afraid we will feel bad, they will be uncomfortable. Eventually they might tend to keep their distance because it is so hard for them to satisfy us.

All this makes it very difficult for someone who feels rejected to have close friends—except for those who have the same problem and want to be comforted in their misery (but this kind of friendship probably won't last long). Another exception might be the exceptionally brave and caring person.

Practical Questions About Rejection

Can you identify with the person who said, "No, I was never good at baseball in school, and everyone seemed to know it. When we chose teams, I was nearly always the last one chosen. In fact, I remember one time when I stood there alone after everyone had been picked, and one captain said to the other, 'You can have him.' The other said, 'Nope; he's yours. You take him.' "

Earlier in this chapter, we learned that the feelings of rejection can be self-inflicted, even if they seem to be based on fact. Does the baseball lineup tell the whole story? Does it reflect your personal worth? Does it speak for every area of your life? No doubt there are things you can do well in. God has given us a variety of sides to our lives—some of which are flatter than others. Surely people are glad to see you show up sometimes!

Maybe we need to take ourselves less seriously. Maybe it's more important to us where we rate in the lineup than it ought to be. Maybe we expect too much of ourselves. Does life owe us the things we were looking for? Did God tell us we should expect to be highly thought of?

When we feel rejected, might the problem be pride? Pride believes it has some rights and is disappointed if these are not honored. Pride will tell you that to be overlooked was an intentional snub. For instance, someone felt deliberately avoided as a possible teacher. Someone who knew the person's feelings investigated the matter, and the school board said, "No, we just didn't think about that person."

But then, what if the rejection is real? People can be thoughtlessly cruel. Some groups have a status system that elevates certain people higher than others. These people are placed above their abilities, while others with more abilities are ignored. And that is not fair; it is not right. It ought not to be in the Christian brotherhood, whether it happens deliberately or by default.

What should be done? Those on the "upper" side of the matter ought to be eager to address the unfairness. Those on the "rejected" side will probably do best by humbly living out the Christian virtues and letting God care for them. "The last shall be first, and the first last" (Matthew 20:16).

By the way, which side would you rather be on? Probably neither, but surely not on the "upper" side, right? We should be like Martin when he was holding a punch to drive out a pin while his partner hit it with a sledgehammer. Something went wrong, and instead of hitting the pin, the hammer mangled Martin's hand. With blood dripping, he had a memorable response: "I would rather you hit me than I hit you."

It is not wrong to ask ourselves whether there are valid reasons why we seem to be passed by. Are there things in your life, your personality, your responses, or your performance that caused it? Responsible positions are usually given to those who have shown sincerity in their lives.

If you frustrate yourself about your station in life, might you be quarreling with God? Might you be saying to the Creator, "Why hast thou made me thus?" The enemy of our souls started his downward course with dissatisfaction. And he is always trying to drag us with him.

Therefore, we don't want to stay on the questioning side. Let's see if there is anything we can do.

Positive Responses

What do the Scriptures recommend to us? How should we look at ourselves?

Jesus said, in Matthew 5:5, "Blessed are the meek." To be meek is to be mild and humble. Are meek people surprised if they are rejected? Are they hurt?

Jesus took the lead in doing what He talked about. In Matthew 11:29, He said, "I am meek and lowly." He was rejected over and over. Luke 9 tells us about a time He was rejected by a village of Samaritans, and His disciples wanted to call fire down from heaven to destroy them. Did Jesus go along with this plan? No; He traveled on, telling His disciples, "Ye know not what manner of spirit ye are of."

Jesus made it clear that man's status measurements are not His. In Luke 13:30, He said, "And, behold, there are last which shall be first, and there are first which shall be last." In God's final analysis, there will be some surprises and some disappointments. Whose approval will we want at the final moment of truth?

No, God does not delight in putting people down and holding them there. Not at all. God wants everyone to take the way down, for that is the way up! Jesus gave us the divine formula in Luke 14:11: "For whosoever exalteth himself shall be abased; and he that humbleth himself shall be exalted."

James 4:10 gives the thought in a similar vein: "Humble yourselves in the sight of the Lord, and he shall lift you up."

We may know all that. But we still want to be useful for God. We are not asking for great things, just the privilege to serve. But somehow the opportunities seem to pass us by.

But wait—do they? The problem can be that we zero in on certain service activities, thinking they are the worthwhile ones. Suppose we are not the organizer, and we think that's too bad. Well, how far could an organizer go without helpers? What would leaders do without followers? Not much! Who is more important—or is that a foolish question?

If you were not given the opportunity you wished for, don't just sit there. Determine to find the joyful way God has for you. Remember that sometimes God uses rejection to redirect us into a better way. No doubt there are lessons to be learned whenever it happens.

Remember too that God never rejects anyone who keeps his eyes on Him. "A friend is one who comes in when all the world has gone out," and God is that friend. Jesus still does what He did to the blind man in John 9:35: "Jesus heard that they had cast him out; and when he had found him . . ." The man was rejected, and Jesus went looking for him—and found him!

No amount of rejection can cut anyone off from the One who takes special interest in us. Nothing can separate any of us from the love of God. Nothing can stop the comforting work of the Holy Spirit. Nothing can rob us from being precious to the One who "hath made us accepted in the beloved" (Ephesians 1:6).

When rejection comes, let's take it in stride and remember that God always has a right and good way for us. God will help us to stay sweet and able to love as we ought. That will melt away the pain of rejection and draw us closer to Him.

Then, by taking God's way, the soul can be free—free indeed!

Chapter Twenty-three

Freedom and Injustice

Injustice is a wrong. It should never have happened. But injustices do happen to everybody. This chapter is about what to do when we are treated wrongly.

Injustices are defining moments of our lives. They show what we are made of and what our true values really are. What is more, they take us up one road or down another.

Joseph was wronged terribly when his brothers hated him and sold him like merchandise. In Egypt he was sold again as a slave. When his master's wife falsely accused him of immorality, his master believed her and threw Joseph into prison. Joseph could have ruined himself in anger and bitterness for the wrong done to him.

But he didn't! Being sold as a slave or being locked up as a criminal could not quench his noble spirit and rob him of his freedom of heart. Instead, he took the high road of patiently doing right. It was years before the full value of his attitude really became apparent.

People still have to wait to be vindicated. Richard was responsible to take care of the money people donated to the food bank. One day someone who had sent cash by mail called and asked for a receipt. But Richard's records had never registered the donation. The cash had simply disappeared. Eyes turned toward Richard. He insisted he was innocent, but had no way to prove it. After several weeks of deep tension, he left his job.

Several weeks after he was gone, he got a call from his former manager, who said they had received the missing letter. It had gotten lost in the mail. The manager apologized profusely for having suspected him. He begged for forgiveness, but Richard would not listen. He still clung to the memory of being falsely accused. His life became darker and darker as he lived and relived the unfairness of it all. He was determined never to be hurt like that again.

The same thing can happen in church. Two members may have a disagreement. Naturally they both feel they are right. They appeal to church leaders, who make disposition of the matter. Being human, the leaders themselves might be in error. The one who was decided against may feel that a gross injustice was done to him. What should he do?

Injustice itself is not the biggest hurt that can be done to the soul. The biggest hurt comes when the soul loses its freedom and languishes in the miserable memory of the wrong done.

Let's think about some of the ways it may happen.

Sources of Injustice

Some things that happen to us are unjust because they are plain wrong. Someone deliberately, obviously trespassed against us, and now we are forced to deal with it.

Other things may not be so wrong as they are unfair. No one harmed us deliberately, but the flow of circumstances brought trouble our way. This has to be dealt with too. Sometimes these circumstances seem more mountainous than they really are.

Regardless of the source or size, our emotional responses to these challenges affect our freedom of heart. Many of the following examples are about incidental matters because we seem to stumble more quickly over them than over obvious ones.

Social injustices. People may be mistreated because of the color of their skin or physical features. People from Africa once suffered much under the cruelties of North Americans. Upright people from Middle Eastern countries have been suspected and arrested because of terrorist concerns. It seems that every society has some sort of social status ladder in which those above mistreat those below.

Abuse of power. Sometimes persons with authority or influence take advantage of others. Children may be abused—physically, mentally, and emotionally. The abuse may come from parents, trusted adults, or influential peers. Children may grow up and mistreat their aged parents. The rich may take advantage of the poor. Multitudes bear deep, deep scars because they were abused in some way. So often, the abused victims turn around and abuse others. What a sad cycle!

Thoughtlessness. Some people suffer from physical deformities. They may be stared at, scoffed at, and separated from the public for things they cannot help or change. Many times, others fail to realize that handicapped people are as human as they are. Perhaps they (or we) haven't gotten close enough to any of them to experience their humanness.

We may mean nothing degrading by it, yet we might tell stories about the antics of a sleepwalking family member. Someone's snoring may be the brunt of entertainment. We may laugh hilariously at the embarrassment of another without realizing how painful it is to the one on whom the spotlight is resting. Even if he is laughing on the outside, he might not be laughing on the inside.

Family injustice. It is hard to treat every family member the same, because circumstances and situations change. The older children may have had to work longer and harder than the younger ones and received less for it because family finances were tight. On the other hand, circumstances may have made it impossible to help the younger children as much as the older ones. The way children respond to these circumstances determines how wounded they will be.

Wrong expectations. We might think more is expected of us than of others, and perhaps that is true. Some people seem to have it easy. Others are loaded down with responsibility. Some have very public positions, where what they do is noticed and applauded, while others labor much harder in secret without recognition. Some are asked to do what others don't want to do. Some are asked to make sacrifices that others are not willing to make. And no one seems to notice. Is it fair?

Unequal opportunities. Although all men were created equal, not all have equal opportunities. This may be because of location or the time in which they live. Some people have financial and service opportunities through family, business, or social contacts. Even though other people may have more abilities, they may not get to use them. God has not promised to give similar circumstances to all.

Neglect. It could be argued that Caleb was overlooked while his partner Joshua was made Moses' heir, even though Caleb was just as faithful. People may be overlooked in a group where responsibilities are generally shared equally. When it seemed to be their turn, someone else was assigned. No one can explain why it happened. It just did.

The list of sad stories could go on and on, but dwelling on them would only make us more miserable. We need to decide what we will allow injustice to do to us.

Symptoms of Responding Wrongly to Injustice

Although injustice can make us more gracious, we must be alert to the symptoms that show we are allowing it to bring our spirits into bondage. This checklist of symptoms indicates wrong responses.

A wounded, offended spirit. Injustice hurts. It tests whether we are ready to take wrongs without giving them back. If we are not willing to forgive, our spirits become calloused and hardened. It puts up walls against those who hurt us. It becomes easy to justify strong feelings toward them. And that opens the door to wrongdoing. Proverbs 18:19 describes how strong the grip becomes and how hard it is to think straight. "A brother offended is harder to be won than a strong city: and their contentions are like the bars of a castle."

Grudging. When a wrong has been done, what should we do about it? We can keep holding it against the offender. And we can nurse the hurt and keep it fresh and tender—like rubbing a new wound. But will that make it better? Someone wisely said, "Most things get better with nursing, but not a grudge."

Grudges are tenacious if hosted. An old friend often said, "You can't keep a grudge without getting it out and looking at it once in a while." Is the memory of the injustice alive and well? Has it affected our thoughts of that person in other ways? If so, the injustice will likely grow so large that we can see little else. Finally, it can paralyze the mind and soul and be a consuming malady. The result is not good.

Anger. No one enjoys being mistreated. People may justify their anger because others have no right to treat them as they do. Anger comes easily when people feel trapped and see no way to escape. They seem to hope that lashing out will help.

Cynicism. Some people are suspicious and critical of everybody. Because someone has wronged them, they feel there is no one they can trust. They dare not let themselves be vulnerable to anyone. They become bitter and sarcastic toward honest efforts of others to do right, because they are sure no one really does right.

Bitterness. Bitterness is like a cancer that eats away on the inside. It shows up first in how we feel, then in how we talk, and finally in what we do. Bitterness has produced calculated murder and other forms of revenge. At the least, it has taken many a person's spirit into captivity. Hebrews 12:15 warns us about how deadly it becomes: "Looking diligently lest any man fail of the grace of God; lest any root of bitterness springing up trouble you, and thereby many be defiled."

Loss of confidence in God. People wonder how and why God allows wrong to go unchecked. Why doesn't someone with authority step in? They wonder why God doesn't deal with it as they think He should—and now!

Sometimes these responses might be looked at as justifiable because of the unfairness that prompted them. But instead of helping the problem, these responses only increase the problem.

One of the ironies of injustice is that its victims often afflict others with similar forms of treatment. A subtle streak of evil in human nature often leads a person to keep alive the very evil he despised in others.

But we are glad for the good news that there is another way. Injustices don't have to ruin us and hold us captive. God has ways to redeem the worst of situations. He gives freedom in the midst of injustice.

Staying Free From the Captivity of Injustice

What shall we do with the injustices that we are aware of? Can we escape or eliminate the sources of injustice? Probably not, because suffering injustice is part of being human. Besides, we ourselves might inflict some injustice on others at times. To try to destroy all injustice would be to destroy ourselves.

Can an injustice be changed? Is it in our power to correct it? Sometimes (and we should if we can), but often there is little to be done from our side. Even if we are the victims, God does not allow us to harbor ill will because of injustice. He has given firm direction on such matters as grudging. "Grudge not one against another, brethren, lest ye be condemned: behold, the judge standeth before the door" (James 5:9).

God has not given us the right to take punitive steps. He said He would take care of matters in His own good time. "Dearly beloved, avenge not yourselves, but rather give place unto wrath: for it is written, Vengeance is mine; I will repay, saith the Lord" (Romans 12:19).

Meanwhile, He gave us the example of Jesus.

Jesus went to the cross in the midst of terrible injustice. He was pure, spotless, and above reproach in every way. Yet His enemies blamed Him for everything they could imagine. And what did He do? He bore it all in regal patience, allowing them to pour out all their hatred and contempt all the way to the cross. First Peter 2:23 summarizes it: "Who, when he was reviled, reviled not again; when he suffered, he threatened not; but committed himself to him that judgeth righteously." And He told us not to be surprised when we experience the same.

Jesus was forsaken by His own disciples. First, Judas betrayed Him. Then the other disciples, in spite of claiming they would not, forsook Him the night before He died. We might find it the same. Being treated wrongly by people who do not care about pleasing God is to be expected. But when it comes from those we know and love and associate with, it hurts deeply. What should we do in such cases?

Jesus directed us on this in Matthew 18. He gave us three steps to follow. Interestingly, He said nothing about our feelings in the matter—it was all to help the one who trespassed. And He made no room to seek any form of retaliation or revenge.

"Moreover if thy brother shall trespass against thee, go and tell him his fault between thee and him alone: if he shall hear thee, thou hast gained thy brother. But if he will not hear thee, then take with thee one or two more, that in the mouth of two or three witnesses every word may be established. And if he shall neglect to hear them, tell it unto the church: but if he neglect to hear the church, let him be unto thee as an heathen man and a publican."

Note again, all of this is for the trespasser's good. This process gives freedom if the heart's desire is for the restoration of the wrongdoer. Galatians 6:1 makes it clear that such matters are for the mature: "Brethren, if a man be overtaken in a fault, ye which are spiritual, restore such an one in the spirit of meekness; considering thyself, lest thou also be tempted."

Your next question might be, "What if no one around me cares enough to carry it this far? I can't round up two or three witnesses!" If you have deposited your concern in the Lord's hands and with those in responsibility, it may be best to leave the matter there. God can bring conviction to hearts in a way that is beyond our comprehension. Meanwhile, don't let it spoil your peace and love.

Jesus endured injustice, not only toward Himself, but also toward others. He heard them putting each other down, and contesting for the top position, and He had some things to say about it. Before we speak too quickly about some injustice, we should pray about it. It may be necessary to share information and concern with those who are able to do something about the situation. Again, it is very important that we do not become emotionally caught up in the problem, but are only concerned for the spiritual good of all.

What if you have been treated wrongly, but others do not see it that way? Should you cry foul, or should you keep quiet? Remember this: how you act about it will affect how seriously others take you. If your response is emotional and negative, others will focus on that rather than on the injustice.

First Peter 2:20 gives us a word on this: "For what glory is it, if, when ye be buffeted for your faults, ye shall take it patiently? But if, when ye do well, and suffer for it, ye take it patiently, this is acceptable with God." Taking it patiently—what a challenge to our spiritual character!

As we noted above, Jesus "committed himself to him that judgeth righteously." Sometimes we need to let God reveal and deal with matters in His own time. It is hard to improve on God's way.

Does that take care of the hurt and tension we might feel about the matter? Not automatically, nor by itself. But if we exercise ourselves to stay in a forgiving frame of mind, the feelings will take care of themselves.

To stay free in the midst of injustice, we must forgive. Not later, but now. Jesus did not wait to forgive until those who crucified Him came and asked for pardon. While they were crucifying Him, He uttered those immortal words, "Father, forgive them; for they know not what they do." Stephen prayed a similar prayer when they stoned him. We cannot have freedom until we forgive! But we have talked about forgiveness before, haven't we.

Obviously, God has used injustices as steppingstones in His own work of providing salvation for us. Now He often uses injustices toward His own to further His own kingdom. So He does not want injustices to become a prison for us. Rather, He wants us to deal with them in the same way our Lord did so that we can be free indeed—even in injustice!

CHAPTER
TWENTY-FOUR

Freedom and the Responsibilities of Life

"Commit thy works unto the LORD, and thy thoughts shall be established" (Proverbs 16:3).

All of us have responsibilities. These responsibilities sometimes create emotional pressures that compete heavily with our joy and freedom.

Ever since seventh grade, Keith had wanted to teach school. When he finally began teaching, he was determined to do a good job—just as his seventh grade teacher had. He wanted the students, the parents, and the board to be happy with his work. Now, after six weeks, he felt weary and burned-out. The workload seemed overwhelming, and the students seemed more listless than he had imagined they could be. What had gone wrong?

Keith decided to call his hero teacher, who was now retired. But the old teacher's mind was not retired. Keith poured out his woes in a torrent. After listening silently for a while, his former teacher asked, "Keith, are you letting the load get you down?"

"Well, I must carry it, mustn't I? What shall I do?"

His teacher was quiet for a while. "Keith, have you ever carried a hundred-pound bag of feed?"

"Of course, I did it all the time on the farm."

"How did you carry it? Did you stretch your arms out and hold the bag as far away from you as you could?"

"No; I put it on my shoulder and kept my body as straight as I could . . . Oh, I see what you are saying! You are telling me I am not carrying my load in the best way, right?"

"Exactly," answered his wise teacher. "That is the problem with many people. The size of the load is not nearly so significant as the way a person carries it. If you hope to survive and do a good job, you must learn to carry your load in a way that gives you freedom in your heart."

Samuel hunched over his checkbook and looked at the bills that were waiting to be paid. "How will it ever reach around?" he moaned. "I thought there would be something left over. I so much wanted to give my family more than this."

His wife put her hand on his shoulder lightly. "My dear husband, we have so much. We have each other, the children, a warm home with enough to eat, and so many spiritual blessings. God is so good. What more could we want?"

Samuel sighed. Slowly his strained face relaxed. He squared his shoulders. "You mean you can be happy the way things are?"

She smiled. "Yes. Why can't you be? You are letting yourself be driven. Can't you trust the Lord? We'd much rather have you, with a free spirit, than have anything else!"

Samuel leaned back in his chair. "Oh, what a relief! I see it now. I was focusing on certain things but overlooking the things that matter the most. I appreciate so much that you helped to lift my eyes to the Lord and His goodness."

The next morning, Samuel went off to work with a fresh spring in his step. He looked forward to the challenges of his work in a new way. He also looked forward more than ever to being at home with his family. How he wanted to be to them what God wanted him to be!

Marie was a busy homemaker. She looked well after her household of a working husband, two schoolchildren, and two preschoolers. She was always available for church activities or to help neighbors. Her warm hospitality drew a constant stream of visitors. She never seemed to run out of energy and optimism.

That was the side most people saw. The other side was exhaustion. She had to push herself from one thing to another. What she wanted to be a joy was a duty. She felt drained. Life was fast becoming one long chore.

These illustrations show that we can become overburdened with good responsibilities to the point that our ability to function is affected. We need the freedom in the line of duty that not only makes us feel better but also enables us to be more efficient and effective.

Let us face some facts.

Responsibilities Are Part of Life

Nobody needs to tell you there are responsibilities in life, but perhaps no one ever told you how many there would be! It is just as well that we can't foresee them all. We must learn to live with them as they come.

Jesus knows that these responsibilities are real. He sympathizes with those under a load. This is His warm invitation: "Come unto me, all ye that labour and are heavy laden, and I will give you rest" (Matthew 11:28). Often He makes the load lighter, but just as often He helps us carry the same load more lightly.

Jesus also warned us that taking on too many responsibilities can become a spiritual threat. "And the cares of this world, [among other things], choke the word, and it becometh unfruitful" (Mark 4:19). Cares are here to stay, and rightly so, but we must beware lest they choke us.

Peter too recognized the reality of cares and told us what to do with them. "Casting all your care upon him; for he careth for you" (1 Peter 5:7).

We do, of course, carry heavy responsibilities. First Timothy 5:8 tells us, "But if any provide not for his own, and specially for those of his own house, he hath denied the faith, and is worse than an infidel." Reneging on these duties carries heavy consequences.

Paul sensed the seriousness of responsibility. God had told him he was "a chosen vessel unto [Him], to bear [His] name before the Gentiles, and kings, and the children of Israel" (Acts 9:15). We know Paul took this responsibility very seriously because he said later, "For though I preach the gospel, I have nothing to glory of: for necessity is laid upon me; yea, woe is unto me, if I preach not the gospel!" (1 Corinthians 9:16).

Responsibilities are not all bad. They can bring the best out of us. Some young people have taken such an easygoing approach that you had to wonder where they would ever go in life. Then something woke them up. This has sometimes happened to young men when they became fathers and suddenly realized what a responsibility they had. Thankfully, they grew up faster than their children, took firm hold of life, and proved themselves faithful.

Responsibilities are God's way of getting things done. We can enjoy them—usually. And what is more fulfilling in life than having been true to the responsibilities we have been given? For Paul, having been true to his calling was high in his mind at the close of his life. "I have fought a good fight, I have finished my course, I have kept the faith" (2 Timothy 4:7).

Now then, how can we face the rigors of responsibility so that we come out at the same end as the apostle Paul did? First, we need to be aware of some snares.

What Responsibilities Can Do to Us

Responsibilities can clutter our minds. Even good responsibilities can come so thick and fast that they are all we can see. If we are not careful, they become like a load of furniture that has just been carried into a house before anything has found its proper place. One's first reaction is, "How will we ever find room for all of this?"

Responsibilities can pressurize our minds. When the pile gets too big, we begin to feel threatened by it. The more threatened we feel, the less intelligently we can make sense of it. Under pressure, we feel as if we were looking for a loose end on a ball of string. We hardly know where to start. We feel we need to do something, but what?

Pressure fosters frustration and impatience. It becomes natural to blame others for our situation. Perhaps we even unduly blame ourselves.

Responsibilities can produce prejudice. Under great responsibility, we tend to lose sight of God's place in our circumstances. This is now *our* project. We perceive things and people to be for *us* or against *us*. We suspect the motives of any persons who seem slow to cooperate with us. (Maybe they are not being obstinate; maybe they just don't know where to help, because we are trying to be everywhere at once.)

Responsibilities can make us feel lonely. To all appearances, some responsibilities are solely our own.

We may carry a weight that no one seems able to share or even care about. That makes responsibilities seem all the more formidable.

"I couldn't find anyone to help me move the machine," a workman mourned, "so I tried to move it myself. Well, that took care of the machine, and me too."

Responsibilities can distract our minds from worthwhile things. They become like clinging burrs or buzzing mosquitoes that occupy the hiker's mind more than anything else he sees. Responsibilities seen in this light will go to the table with us and spoil our meal and the table atmosphere. They will go to bed with us and hinder our sleep. They will even go to church if allowed and hinder our concentration and ability to worship.

When these things happen, freedom deteriorates.

What Can Be Done?

Here are some practical suggestions.

Determine what your responsibilities are. We are surrounded by things which we could do and would like to do. We can easily end up feeling that we ought to carry the whole world on our shoulders. An overburdened person takes a giant step in the right direction when it dawns on him that many things he felt responsible for were not really his God-given responsibility. According to John 5:1–9, even Jesus did not heal every sick person He saw.

Be realistic about what you can do. Yes, it would be nice to do many things, but it may not be possible to do them all now—and it may be hard to do them properly! When we expect too much, it is hard to appreciate what we do get done.

Divide responsibilities into manageable parts. Could you eat an elephant? No? Someone told me you can eat an elephant if you cut it into small enough pieces. (Just don't try to do it all at once!) Do one thing at a time. It can help to unlock your mind and get it functioning.

Establish priorities. Which of our responsibilities is most urgent? Which will prove to be the most important five years from now? One minister was struggling about whether to harvest his crop on Saturday or prepare to preach the next day. He finally said, "It is better if we go hungry than if the congregation goes hungry tomorrow." He had it straight, didn't he.

Share responsibilities when possible. Sometimes we can help ourselves by delegating responsibility or asking someone else to help. It may be refreshing to discover how much help is available if we are willing to ask—and accept it!

Try to reduce your workload. Some duties are ours, pure and simple. Some others we may have taken on out of interest in being helpful. Some we may have taken because we did not say no when we should have.

We should be careful when and how we say no. Childish laziness might still be haunting us. Sometimes after we say yes when we felt like saying no, time proves that we said the right thing. But there are times and places to say no without feeling guilty.

Reach out to others who have similar workloads. The fact that we are not alone in a project encourages us. Notice how often people in these situations have become fast friends and helped each other along. And it was not only because misery loves company!

Let others in on your burdens. This is true not only of workloads but also of the pains and disappointments of life. There is great strength in knowing other people care and are eager to share.

These have been mostly practical hints to help you lighten the load. But what if the load cannot be lightened?

Freedom Under the Load

We can only have free spirits in the responsibilities of life by letting the Lord help us to bear them. He is more than willing; the question is whether or not we are working with Him.

Freedom when responsibilities increase. Matthew 25:14–30 tells the parable of the talents. To each of his servants, the lord gave some form of money. He expected them to use these talents and to do well with them in his absence. Upon returning, he rewarded those who handled their responsibilities well by giving them more. So it is with Christian service—the reward for responsibilities well done is more of the same. And so the cycle repeats itself over and over again.

But with the increasing responsibilities comes increased pressure. Yet God has wonderfully created us to be His servants and made serving Him a fulfilling, rewarding, and even joyful thing. The lord in the parable told the faithful servants, "Thou hast been faithful over a few things, I will make thee ruler over many things: enter thou into the joy of thy lord." Did you catch that? "Enter thou into the joy of thy lord." Apparently, the wise handling of responsibility brings more responsibility—and with that, more joy. "The service of Jesus true pleasure affords."

What Nehemiah 8:10 tells us applies here—"The joy of the LORD is your strength." While faithfulness in existing responsibility may bring more responsibility, it is the joy of the Lord that strengthens us for the work.

The entire process of responsibilities, work, strength, and joy, is in the Lord's control. Depending on Him and being among His happy servants give freedom, even though the workload may seem heavy.

Freedom comes by committing every area of our lives to God. Yes, we have interests and desires, but we trust the outworking of them to Him. We need to live in strong faith that Romans 8:28 is still at work: God can always make good come out of every part of life. "And we know that all things work together for good to them that love God, to them who are the called according to his purpose."

When we are living for God, our lives are His lives and our work is His work. We can then say the same thing Paul did, in 2 Timothy 1:12: "For I know whom I have believed, and am persuaded that he is able to keep that which I have committed unto him against that day." He does the keeping; we do the committing.

Freedom is for those who live sincerely before God. At times our best efforts at serving the Lord fail miserably. Can we rest in the knowledge that God knows our hearts and is well aware of what we want to do? First John 3:20 says, "God is greater than our heart, and knoweth all things." The poet said, "Not what I did, but what I strove to do." This thought needs to be kept within proper limits, but it can be of strengthening comfort to us at those times.

Freedom is possible for those who are yoked with Christ. What Jesus said in Matthew 11 bears repeating: "Take my yoke upon you, and learn of me; for I am meek and lowly in heart: and ye shall find rest unto your souls. For my yoke is easy, and my burden is light." Where Jesus is, everything is under control. In the storms of life, Jesus is able to do what He did to the storms at sea. "Peace!" He says. "Be still."

There is no substitute for a close, warm walk with God. We must be in constant touch with Him. When we have His peace and rest in our hearts, we can see life in its proper perspective. Then we can be free indeed!

"If the Son therefore shall make you free, ye shall be free indeed."

Chapter
Twenty-five

Freedom in Stress and Fatigue

"My heart panteth, my strength faileth me: as for the light of mine eyes, it also is gone from me" (Psalm 38:10).

The doctor decided to give me a stress test for my heart. They wired me up in about a dozen places and put me on a treadmill to see what I could take. They warned me that it was going to be a stressful stress test.

It was. They kept turning up the speed of the belt I was walking on, faster and faster. They made me keep on and on until I thought I would drop over. But the doctor would not let me stop. He kept me going until I was totally exhausted. Finally it was over.

Sometimes our emotions are like that. They can put our minds on an emotional treadmill. We feel like we are close to our maximum endurance level. We wonder how to go on.

Is this kind of sensation new? Actually, Job told us about this a long time ago. "Man that is born of a woman is of few days, and full of trouble" (Job 14:1). Needless to say, he experienced lots of stress in his life!

The psalmist paints a similar picture in Psalm 38: "I am troubled; I am bowed down greatly; I go mourning all the day long. . . . I am feeble and sore broken: I have roared by reason of the disquietness of my heart. Lord, all my desire is before thee; and my groaning is not hid from thee. My heart panteth, my strength faileth me: as for the light of mine eyes, it also is gone from me."

Was the psalmist fighting God? No; he was reaching out to Him. The last two verses of the psalm say, "Forsake me not, O LORD: O my God, be not far from me. Make haste to help me, O Lord my salvation." In Psalm 142:7, he said, "Bring my soul out of prison."

Another time the psalmist compared himself to a deer—a terrified deer running for its life and now desperately thirsty: "As the hart panteth after the water brooks, so panteth my soul after thee, O God" (Psalm 42:1). *Panteth* does not suggest a leisurely Sunday afternoon walk in the woods. It displays urgency. That is how needy he felt toward God.

Stress, such as Job and David experienced, is a fact of life. Sometimes people wish for the "good old stress-free days." Were early civilizations stress-free when the people eked out a living from uncooperative soil and dealt with harsh climates? Were the pioneers free from stress when a slipped-ax wound could cause bleeding to death and the life expectancy was barely more than forty years? Stress is not a new thing at all.

Stress is usually considered to be a hindrance to our well-being. Let's evaluate that.

Is Stress Always Bad?

Stress helps us do what we never thought we could do. It has been proven that a man being chased by a bear can run faster and longer than he ever dreamed he could. Someone explaining why a dog could not catch a rabbit said that the dog was only running for his lunch—the rabbit was running for his life!

When Hurricane Agnes dumped torrential rains on our community, the floodwaters rose very rapidly. We went through the neighborhood and helped each other get things out of the basements. We carried out loaded freezers that we would not have even tried to carry on a nice, sunny day. Many things much more noble than this have been done under stress which could never have been done without stress.

Stress can sharpen our concentration. The right amount of stress helps us to stay alert under bad road conditions. It counteracts carelessness and overconfidence.

The stress of earning a livelihood makes us want to have a job. The stress of keeping the job helps us stay on our toes. It helps us to be productive.

The point is that stress should not be despised, because it is not all bad. It can help bring the good out of us. Some people actually thrive on a high degree of stress.

However, as with anything else, too much stress can be damaging. Driving a horse too hard can ruin it. Gripping the steering wheel until the knuckles are white shows that the driver is under too much stress for safe driving. Ignoring one's own stress levels can bring physical and emotional calamity. "You're burning the candle at both ends," a young wife observed to her husband. He just laughed. But the laughing ended when his health collapsed.

Do these principles apply to the spirit as well? Can stress sharpen and stretch our faith? On the other hand, will too much stress injure it?

Think about the heroes of faith in Hebrews 11. Did Abraham experience any stress when he was told to slay his son? Did Moses' parents feel any stress when they slipped his basket into the Nile? Did Rahab sense any stress while the walls of Jericho were falling? No doubt they did, but their faith helped to keep their stress level from going off the graph, and they triumphed.

But if stress comes too heavy and too fast for us to handle, it raises serious challenges to our whole being. It can put pressure on our emotions that can make faith difficult. It then takes away the joy of living and our ability to draw encouragement from God.

Causes of Overstress

Not accepting normal stresses can quickly cause overstress. Children get sick, the car breaks down, the bread flops. Yesterday a friend had to stay home from work to fix his water pump in his house. Then he had to work in the evening to stay current with his job. He could say, "Well, that's just how life is," or he could ask, "Why are all these things happening to me?" One way he is fine; the other way he is heading for emotional difficulties.

Major disappointments can cause considerable stress if we did not allow for them in our vision for the future. The death of an infant, a dashed dream, the failure of someone we trusted (or a failure of our own) will affect us in ways we need to come to terms with.

Overtaxing or overextending ourselves can raise the stress level. We can bring this on by committing ourselves to workloads or deadlines that are well-nigh impossible. We can do it by overextending our finances and earning power. Even if these things are all for a good cause, they take their toll—likely at the home and spiritual level.

We can create stress by being overly determined to do what we set out to do. If we schedule ourselves in such a way that everything has to click exceptionally well, we are asking for stress—especially if we are determined to end up with an exceptionally good product!

Taking overly serious concern about life generates stress. We can end up trying to carry the world on our shoulders. If we take our concerns along to bed, to work, and to church, they can become so intense that they crowd out simple faith and trust in God.

Asking too much from life generates stress. We tend to think that life owes us certain things. We can even feel that we should achieve the same objectives our friends and neighbors have attained. We may feel that happiness comes by achieving certain goals, such as getting married, owning a home, gaining financial security, and maintaining good health. Trying to achieve these just because we think life owes them to us brings tension to us and those around us.

Unresolved problems cause stress. The more of them that accumulate, the more stress they cause. If we let them pile up unresolved, they often fall on us at the wrong time in the wrong way.

Feeling alone with our problems adds to stress. Ironically, many of us find that when we need people the most, we are most tempted to pull away from everyone and go hide in a hole!

Weariness causes stress. When we are tired, our difficulties are magnified. Often weariness comes as a result of our own bad management. We have allowed our outgo to exceed our input for too long. We have created a sleep debt or a refreshment debt. As a result, we suffer physically, emotionally, and spiritually.

Human relationships can be stressful. When we have a disagreement or a misunderstanding with someone, we feel it. When communication has broken down and those once close to us seem far away, it hurts. When we feel that we have tried so hard to have good relationships, it is disappointing to have others turn their backs on us. Of course, if we know we have not tried as hard as we should, that causes even more stress.

We each need to develop our early-warning systems to watch for the things that cause more stress than we are able to handle. We need to learn to say no or to back away if we sense that a situation will put us in difficulties we cannot handle. We need not feel bad when others seem to have higher endurance levels than we do. God did not create us all alike.

Glancing back over the causes of stress leads us to realize that usually the greatest cause of stress is within us. Stress results from how we look at things! Tension naturally rises if we let our emotions run.

When we let our emotions go where they will, they become negative and they dredge up dark, foreboding thoughts. They bring up bad memories that we thought were behind us. Past failures of our own, or more likely of others, race through our minds and make it harder to see the present situation as we ought.

How do we know when we are pushing the line?

Evidences of Overstress

Sometimes our stress overload is more evident to people around us than to ourselves. We can make it easier for others and ourselves if we note the evidence and respond accordingly.

We will let the psalmist continue to diagnose his stress level by recognizing his own symptoms in Psalm 42.

Lack of joy. The psalmist said he was constantly in tears. A friend once told me, "I felt so sad on the inside." Another said, "I felt like crying all the time." A man visiting a church service stood up and demanded of the audience,

"Where is your joy?" Maybe everyone was a little stressed that day. Hopefully, as one man suggested, "We are happier than we look!"

The tendency to complain. The psalmist said, "I pour out my soul in me. . . . My soul is cast down within me." When we find it hard to be satisfied with what others do or with our circumstances, watch out.

Loneliness. The psalmist put the question to God, "Why hast thou forgotten me?" When we feel no one cares and we don't know where to turn, we need to think again.

Despair. The psalmist complained of "a sword in [his] bones." The apostle Paul said, "We were pressed out of measure, above strength, insomuch that we despaired even of life" (2 Corinthians 1:8).

What can we expect if stress continues?

The Crippling Effects of Too Much Stress

Lack of concentration. Stress can preoccupy the mind. It is said that the traffic accident rate goes up for people who have just lost a loved one. Evidently they are too preoccupied to pay proper attention to the road. Stress can make it especially hard to concentrate on spiritual things. It distracts the mind during personal Bible reading and prayer. It goes along to church and interferes with true participation in worship.

When stress overruns us, it multiplies our problems. It says, "Everything went wrong" or "It never . . ." or "It always . . ." It tends to compose an extreme, worst-case scenario. Someone feeling the first twinges of arthritis might wonder how soon he will find himself in a wheelchair—or he might interpret every ache as a terminal illness.

Emotionalism. Stress can affect the emotions to the point that the emotions control the will. When feelings become our master, they keep us from sleeping well. They make it hard for us to go to bed, to get out of bed, to get on with work, and to look on the bright side of life. Truly, they can keep the soul in prison.

Indecision. Stress can paralyze the mind and hinder us in making decisions. As our problems churn in our minds, they become intimidating and confusing. The mind then tends to lunge here and there in an effort to alleviate the stress and solve the cause. But alas, even the decisions we try to make seem to mock us.

For instance, a friend of mine needed some plumbing done in a house he had bought. But his stress was so high that he couldn't make himself call the plumber! Finally, after about two weeks of indecision, which only made things worse, he simply grabbed the telephone one day and called. Stress makes indecision, but indecision increases stress. This can be a vicious, never-ending cycle. Obviously, he wished he had done it sooner.

Loss of physical strength. The tension of trying to anticipate everything before it happens absorbs an enormous amount of energy, causing physical weariness. A cruel cycle can develop because physical weariness in turn can weaken emotional buoyancy, subjecting the sufferer to even more tension. "The joy of the LORD is your strength" works in reverse, if we allow it.

Exhaustion. Sometimes exhaustion is called burnout, which is the result of long-term stress. The question is whether it is real or imagined. Here is what one teacher said to another: "Did you ever feel as if you were burning out? Any person in a high-stress job, such as teaching, faces that possibility. If you are facing some personal stress in addition to your job stress, you may be a candidate for burning out. On the other hand, anyone with a high-stress job, like teaching, will face times when he feels burned out. You may simply be suffering from stress reaction." How could he know?

We all have to live with our own emotions. We cannot make them go away by merely ignoring them, so we might as well learn to work with them. Of course, we need to be careful not to take them so seriously that we pamper ourselves.

What can we do to work with the evidences of stress?

Coping With Stress

At a teachers' meeting, I heard an experienced teacher give his testimony about a time he thought he was almost burned out. He was having a difficult time at school, evidently. Since they had a new baby in their family, he was doing a lot of extra work at home as well as getting up at five o'clock to study for school. The work and lack of sleep finally got to him, and he simply could not take it anymore.

His solution? He went to bed at seven o'clock that evening and slept for twelve hours. The world looked different when he woke up. The night before, he thought he was burning out. The next morning, he realized he just had not had enough sleep!

Since stress is here to stay and we cannot always prevent it, we need to look for ways to cope with it.

The psalmist did more than spew out his troubles. He got out of the jungle he was in. Let's follow his signposts.

Be fair. In Psalm 42:5, he raised both sides of the matter. He addressed his own problem and then gave himself a good answer. "Why art thou cast down, O my soul? and why art thou disquieted in me? hope thou in God: for I shall yet praise him for the help of his countenance."

Remember. A verse later, he said, "I remember . . ." It was a short, simple statement, but helpful. He remembered the faithfulness of God and all the past things that helped him to have confidence in God now. He then reaffirmed his confidence in God: "Yet the LORD will command his lovingkindness in the daytime, and in the night his song shall be with me, and my prayer unto the God of my life."

Have faith. More than once, the psalmist said to himself, "Hope thou in God." We need not try to disbelieve our troubles. We need not try to prevent them with the assurance that "everything will be all right." All we need is to stop holding our breath and rest in the confidence that God is good.

Be thankful. Reckon with the negatives, certainly, but focus on the good things. You will only invite stress if you major on the negatives and forget to thank God for all He has done for you and for all the large and small reassurances that He has not forgotten you.

Resign everything to God. Stress may come while we are working toward legitimate dreams, ideas, and plans. When they elude us and don't work out, what should we do? Fight it or accept it? The only way to have rest is to surrender all to God.

Establish priorities. The ambulance crew that comes to the scene of an accident in which several people need help has to decide whom to help first. A high-stress situation? Certainly. But deciding beforehand that serious bleeding gets the first attention, that the suspected heart attack gets the next, and the broken bones get help later does much to alleviate stress.

Sometimes when our families need attention, we need to say about other things, "They don't matter" or "They can wait." Our time with our families will then be of higher quality than if we spend our family time stewing over some other project that we consider equally important. "Oh, where is the mother whose house is so shocking? / She's up in the nursery, blissfully rocking" may be oversimplified, but it illustrates the point.

It's easy for me to think some things must be done now. But someone asks, "Are you sure?" "Well, yes . . . well . . . maybe not . . . let's see . . ." And then I realize it is not as pressing as I thought. That relieves lots of pressure that was of my own making.

Compare. It is easy to think we have it hard in life. But when we compare ourselves fairly with others, we realize that we are better off than many others.

> I had the blues
> Because I had no shoes
> Until I met upon the street
> A man who had no feet.

What if this book falls into the hands of the person whose troubles are worse than anyone else's in the world? (Such a person has to exist somewhere, and maybe you are the one!) You might do like one man whose hand was caught in a corn picker. While in agonizing pain, he thought of Christ on the cross and prayed for every lost soul he could think of.

We might also compare our present situation to the record of the past. The law of averages would show that we have been in similar situations before, but it all worked out in the long run, many times better than we thought it would.

Finally, nothing summarizes this chapter better than the familiar old "Prayer of Serenity."

> God, grant me the serenity
> To accept the things I cannot change,
> Courage to change the things I can,
> And the wisdom to know the difference.

CHAPTER
TWENTY-SIX

Freedom and Contentment

"Be content with such things as ye have: for he hath said, I will never leave thee, nor forsake thee" (Hebrews 13:5).

Contentment is sweet balm for the soul. It has liberating power because its needs are satisfied. It breathes the cool, fresh air of thankfulness.

On the other hand, discontentment enslaves. It covets that which it does not have. It confines the spirit with self-pity because it believes that satisfaction lies in what it craves. It has always been one of Satan's most effective ways to bring men and women into his grip.

Adam and Eve originally had everything the heart could wish for. Genesis 2:16, 17 tells us that God restricted them from only one tree in the beautiful Garden of Eden. Satan used that one tree to ensnare them. Eve started admiring the tree wistfully. She thought about the beauty and the deliciousness of that fruit. The more she looked and thought, the more she wanted it.

Soon she became discontented. Instead of thinking of all she had in the Garden (had she yet tasted of all the other trees?), she thought about what she couldn't have. She looked at the forbidden tree and saw how pleasant it looked and thought about how desirable it was. Eventually she ate of the forbidden fruit, and the human race has been infested with discontentment ever since. Can you identify with these examples?

Calvin drove past the same used-vehicle lot every day he went to work. One morning a dark blue pickup was on the special-for-the-week display. It was everything a man could wish for in a truck. He looked and turned to look again. As he drove on, he started looking at his own truck. Suddenly he noticed a strange noise in the engine. He heard some new rattles.

On the way home from work, Calvin wondered if that truck was still there. It was. He slowed down. Should he stop? Deep down, he knew he could not afford it. And, just several weeks ago, he had told the other men at work what a good truck he had. But it seemed as if gravity drew him into the sales lot. He walked around the truck several times and started getting back into his own. His mind was in a whirl. All the way home, he thought about how bad his truck was and how good the other one was.

"What's on your mind?" Calvin's wife asked after supper. "You act like you're in a daze."

Calvin flushed. "Why, uh, I saw a truck for sale that is just what I need. You know, ours is getting fairly old, and—and— "

His wife looked at him blankly, and he ground to an embarrassed halt.

After a few moments, he smiled. "It looks like I fell into the trap of discontentment. Really, our truck is good enough, isn't it."

Another wise wife faced the same thing with her husband. She suggested that he sweep out his truck, wash the windows, and wipe the dashboard. He was amazed how that helped to deliver him from his discontentment and to appreciate what he had.

"How can you stand living in such an old house?" Hannah's eyes swept the old kitchen again.

"What do you mean?" Marie smiled. "I have been to places where people did not have it nearly this nice. And besides, we are perfectly happy here. Or do you think I would be happier in your house?"

Hannah's eyes fell. She was silent, and her eyes glistened with tears. "I must admit that you are happier in your house than I am in mine. I must go."

Theodore listened quietly as his friends talked about how much money they were making at their jobs. Even more exciting was what they said they were going to do with their money. He had nothing to say.

"Why are you so quiet, son?" his father asked on the way home. "Is something wrong?"

Theodore squirmed. "Well, it's just that when I hear my friends talk about their jobs and their money, I feel stuck here on the farm. Usually I like it and would not trade with any of them; but sometimes I, uh . . ."

"And which times do you feel the best, son?" Father queried. "Which do you really want?"

Slowly Theodore brightened. "I am happy where I am. I just needed to hear that."

Tracing the spirits of these examples shows us that happiness and freedom of heart do not lie in having everything we might wish for. They lie in being content and satisfied where we are and in being able to see the good right there.

How Discontentment Enslaves

In a revealing story called "Ring Around a Rosy," a well-to-do couple got tired of living in New York and decided to move to England. They took up residence in the home of a couple who was tired of England and had moved to Italy. In Italy, the English couple leased a villa from a man who was tired of Italy and was moving to Germany. In Germany, the Italian found a home in the house of a couple who was tired of Germany and was moving to America. In New York, the German couple found the very home of the American couple who had left for England. They were delighted with their New York home (though the wife suggested that sometime soon they might go live in China!).

That is how some people are! If a move is necessary, however, how good when people can move from place to place and enjoy each spot for what it is. But how much better when they are not driven from one place to another just to satisfy the yearning of discontentment.

When we are not content, we become critical of our circumstances. Whether we are discontented with our houses, our jobs, our vehicles, or with life itself, our difficulties and disadvantages tend to escalate. We figure that other people have it so much better. The more we think about it, the worse we feel. When we are caught in the trap of discontentment, our thinking is no longer realistic. We constantly imagine how happy we would be if we had the things we do not have, and we forget the blessings we do have.

Discontentment seems to thrive on misery. It doesn't really want to be happy. How do we know? Give discontentment what it wants now, and it will soon want more!

Discontentment fosters envy. It makes it painful for us to see others with the privileges we would like to have. It becomes easy to criticize them for enjoying the very things we would like to enjoy ourselves. Envy even points out the supposedly unfair methods they used to obtain the possessions or privileges they have, and how they misuse them. All these things underscore how unfair life has been to us!

Discontentment has robbed people of jobs, properties, friends, homes, and many other things because they left what they had, to follow a mirage. Many people have said remorsefully—but too late—that they should have stayed where they once were and kept what they once had. A book about some local people like this was aptly titled *Rainbow Chasers*.

Discontentment causes people to reason themselves out of relationships. Husbands and wives may become discontented with their homes and with each other. Their unhealthy thoughts, if not checked, can cause them to drift apart. Many who have taken this course and gone on to other relationships probably realize eventually that they would not have had to choose the way they did. But usually they realize it only after untold and irreparable damage has been done.

Some people become discontented with their church. Granted, there are churches one should not be satisfied with. However, members of Scriptural churches have sometimes become frustrated and discontented and finally reasoned themselves into a state of mind that led them away into places they thought they would never go. Many end up accepting things far more objectionable than what put them on the move in the first place. And others may have found themselves where God wanted them to be, but were asking, "Why doesn't anyone ever address the problems that frustrate people in the first place?" Some of these people started out with honest concerns that were not resolved and ended up being discontented—and thus unable to help the situation.

Eventually, discontented people have a hard time being content with God. Even *He* doesn't always do what they think He should. Whose fault is my poor health? or my lot in life? or my family's poverty? Whose fault is it that other people have all the good opportunities? And who is easier to blame for these things than God!

As we can see, discontentment is a deep, deep pit. Its iron grip must be broken. Thank God it can be!

How Contentment Gives Us Freedom

The secret of contentment is not in having everything we want but in wanting what we have. It is in being satisfied where we are and with what we have. It helps us to be free because we appreciate our circumstances. Men who are content don't need to turn their heads when they pass used-car lots. Wives who are content don't need to spend their time dreaming about what all else their houses should have. Young men who are content are not constantly wishing they could trade places with others.

Contentment lies in believing that God is involved in our lives for our good and that He is always working to bring glory to Himself through His children. Contentment then produces deep satisfaction.

The following verses show that contentment does not lie in things but rather in living in God's ways.

"A little that a righteous man hath is better than the riches of many wicked" (Psalm 37:16).

"Remove far from me vanity and lies: give me neither poverty nor riches; feed me with food convenient for me: lest I be full, and deny thee, and say, Who is the LORD? or lest I be poor, and steal, and take the name of my God in vain" (Proverbs 30:8, 9).

"But godliness with contentment is great gain" (1 Timothy 6:6).

God is more interested in holy contentment than in possessions. Are possessions wrong? No; but the desire for possessions has led many people the wrong way. The state of mind and the actions of discontented people are more wrong than the possessions they might buy. Here are several verses that explain what happens if we are not content.

"And having food and raiment let us be therewith content. But they that will be rich fall into temptation and a snare, and into many foolish and hurtful lusts, which drown men in destruction and perdition. For the love of money is the root of all evil: which while some coveted after, they have erred from the faith, and pierced themselves through with many sorrows" (1 Timothy 6:8–10).

Note that it is the "will" to be rich and "the love of money" that take people the wrong way. True freedom comes from desiring the things of God rather than the things of this life.

"Let your conversation be without covetousness; and be content with such things as ye have: for he hath said, I will never leave thee, nor forsake thee. So that we may boldly say, The Lord is my helper, and I will not fear what man shall do unto me" (Hebrews 13:5, 6).

Contentment does not come naturally. Sometimes it must be learned—and likely relearned. The apostle Paul tells how he had to learn it.

"Not that I speak in respect of want: for I have learned, in whatsoever state I am, therewith to be content. I know both how to be abased, and I know how to abound: every where and in all things I am instructed both to be full and to be hungry, both to abound and to suffer need" (Philippians 4:11, 12).

Evidently Paul understood that both fullness and hunger are good if they come from the hand of God, and that was good enough for Him. If we have God, it doesn't matter what else we don't have; and if we do not have God, it doesn't matter what else we do have.

Another major key to contentment is thankfulness. The Bible, in numerous places, calls us to be thankful. For example, Colossians 3, in directing Christians how to live, says, "And be ye thankful." Why? Because there is so much for believers to be thankful for.

Discontentment and thankfulness can't live together. They don't mesh. But contentment and thankfulness are an indomitable pair. They can help you have freedom!

As you can see, the freedom of contentment is within reach!

Chapter
Twenty-seven

Freedom and Perfectionism

Perfectionism is the feeling we must be perfect in all that we do. Trying to be perfect is good. It adds interest and zest to our jobs. The problem is that no one really achieves absolute perfection. And likely, those who get the closest to it would be the last to consider themselves perfect.

The painter sees the flaws on his own canvas most quickly. And the skilled craftsman in the body shop sees all his own flaws in the cars he fixes. So does every other craftsman or craftswoman, from mechanic to cook.

Although trying to be perfect is a good goal, perfectionism is a step beyond that—a long, cruel, punishing step. Perfectionists have a very hard time ever being satisfied. Trying to do everything perfectly puts enormous pressure on the soul. It affects our inner peace and joy. It makes what could be enjoyable become a burden. And, as you have probably discovered, sometimes it seems the harder we try to do something perfectly, the worse we do at it. Hopefully, working through this problem will help us to function with freedom—and maybe even come closer to our goals!

Glenn was a painter. He took the challenge of doing a good job very seriously. He could not tolerate any blemishes. His employer appreciated his conscientious, hard work because he knew he never had to worry about whether the job was done right. What he did not know was that Glenn was constantly tied in knots because he could not stand it if the job was not absolutely perfect. Even though the job was good by industry standards, he still had a hard time deciding to let it be good enough and to move on. By the end of the day, Glenn was more tired from trying to decide when it was good enough than he was from the work itself. He decided to talk to his employer about it.

His employer listened quietly. "Why, Glenn," he said, "I don't expect absolute perfection, because it really isn't possible. Yes, our customers expect a good job, but don't punish yourself if there are a few brush marks or something like that when you are done. And look, I'll tell you if something is not satisfactory. Just move forward."

Glenn sighed with relief. "Thank you. I think that will be easier for me. I do want to do good work. But I'll let you be the judge!"

If we have a perfectionist-prone personality, anything we do has the potential to trouble us in this way. When is something good enough? When should we be satisfied and go on? Many things could be done better. How much pressure should such concerns put on us? On the other hand, we should not use this as an excuse to do careless work.

Perfectionism can create a problem by harassing us spiritually. We can become so critical of ourselves that we intensify our own difficulties. True, some people ought to care more about themselves; they settle for far less than they should. Rather than criticizing them at length, let's think about ourselves.

"Anita, what's wrong with you this morning?" Wanda queried her co-worker.

Anita sighed. "My devotional life. I determined last week to have the kind of devotions that really fueled me up for the day. But it doesn't seem to work that way at all. My devotions have gotten more dull instead."

Wanda leaned against the door. "What did you read today? Did you get spiritual food? Was there anything for you to take with you? Did you commit yourself and your day to the Lord?"

"Of course I did. But it didn't give me the spiritual boost I hoped for." Anita sighed again.

"Are you sure you're not expecting too much? Maybe you're looking for something that you hoped would put you in the clouds, above the daily struggles of life. But life is real. I had to come to grips with that too," Wanda concluded. "Relax and rejoice in the Lord."

Perfectionism can discourage us in trying to do good things well.

"Ethan, what are you doing out here?" Andrew asked as he stooped to look into the car window after church. "Why do you look so glum?"

"Oh, it's the Sunday school class," Ethan mumbled. "It went so poorly. I won't ever teach again. I had studied hard and was determined to have a good class, but it was a flop. I got out of there as quickly as I could."

"Ethan, that's not true. I was in the class, and I not only enjoyed it but was greatly challenged by it. Come on in."

Once again, don't misunderstand me. It is right to want to do a good job at anything we do. We ought to find satisfaction in seeing results from our efforts. But the problems show up when we don't know where to stop, and don't understand what is driving us.

Problems of Perfectionism

Perfectionism creates unrealistic expectations. If we were perfect and lived in a perfect world, we would quite naturally expect perfection from ourselves and everyone else. But when we expect perfection in this imperfect world, we are setting ourselves up for disappointment. What are we to do with the inevitable shortfall?

Some people resolve the shortfall by quitting. The "If I can't do it perfectly, I won't do it at all" attitude is destructive because practically everything we do must be learned over a period of time and improved upon. If perfectionism prevails, it will get in the way of getting better.

Perfectionism takes away the joy and satisfaction of present progress. "You did that one quite well!" "Yes, but wait till you see the next one I'll do." Or "It's not as good as you think. Look here . . ."

Perfectionism wastes time. It wants to tinker and fine-tune endlessly. It finds it hard to move on. Whether we are builders or seamstresses, there is a time to move on. Even editors face that problem when working on manuscripts.

Perfectionism makes it difficult for us to accept ourselves. It creates a punishing, judgmental attitude toward oneself, which makes life miserable. The self-consciousness it generates makes the sufferer overly sensitive to what others might think—or what we think they might be thinking.

One person said, "When I was twenty, I worried what others were thinking of me. When I was forty, I didn't care what they were thinking of me. When I reached sixty, I realized that they hadn't been thinking of me at all!"

Perfectionism makes it hard for us to be thankful and appreciative of our circumstances. If things are not exactly right, it is hard for us to see the good in them because all we can see is what could be better or what should be fixed. The perfectionist's focus is constantly on what should yet be rather than on what is. The connection between being thankful and being happy and free can't be ignored.

Perfectionism might not be so bad if we were only perfectionistic about ourselves. But we tend to view others through the same magnifying glasses. We can easily become intolerant of others and never quite satisfied with them. We can expect more of them than of ourselves. And that puts pressure on them and us!

Some of us remember thinking that our parents were never quite satisfied when they looked at our school report cards. It seemed to me that my father saw only the grades that could have been better instead of the A's that I thought I worked so hard for. But then, our children felt the same way when we looked at their report cards! Perhaps some perfectionist parents should compare their children's report cards with their own.

Perfectionism can be very discouraging. Some children who could never do things quite well enough for their parents have struggles accepting themselves later in life. They lack confidence and are afraid to take the initiative. Oftentimes they have a problem appreciating their parents because the parents don't live up to their own perfectionism.

Perfectionism and realism—which is which? How and when should we do our best and let it rest? That is a lifetime of discovery!

Perfectionism and Pride

The possibility that perfectionism might be pride must be considered. Why do we want to do so well? Is it because we want the attention and approval of others? Is it because we want to be a cut above the rest? Is it an image issue? These are sobering questions that we each can answer only for ourselves.

Was Glenn's problem a sincere interest in his work? or was he trying to live up to a reputation he wanted to have? Was Anita's frustration honest? or was she trying to be a super Christian, better than anyone else? Was Ethan suffering from a real sense of utter failure? or was he nursing wounded pride? And why was I disappointed when my parents didn't applaud my good grades? Who can tell? The bigger issue now is how we deal with these matters.

If the perfectionist thinks he has at last reached the peak of his potential, his pride will show. How? Quite likely, he will compare himself with others of less achievement and show a competitive spirit toward those who excel. The perfectionist can end up without a friend in the world. "It's lonely at the top," especially if "the top" is one you have created for yourself.

We need to look for ways to deal with these difficulties.

Finding Freedom From Perfectionism

The first step in dealing with perfectionism is to realize what God expects.

When God called the apostle Paul, He described him thus: "He is a chosen vessel unto me, to bear my name before the Gentiles, and kings, and the children of Israel: for I will shew him how great things he must suffer for my name's sake" (Acts 9:15, 16).

What a high calling! And Paul gave himself to it totally. How did Paul feel about it? Was he driven day and night to reach that calling? Did he feel responsible to be perfect in it all?

Here is how he looked at himself: "Not as though I had already attained, either were already perfect: but I follow after, if that I may apprehend that for which also I am apprehended of Christ Jesus. Brethren, I count not myself to have apprehended: but this one thing I do, forgetting those things which are behind, and reaching forth unto those things which are before, I press toward the mark for the prize of the high calling of God in Christ Jesus" (Philippians 3:12–14).

Paul did not pretend to be perfect in achievement. He said he kept pressing toward the mark. Did he expect to reach it in this life? Hardly, because he always saw new horizons stretching out before him. Nevertheless, he was free in his heart because he was moving with God.

That is where freedom is for us too. Emotional freedom lies in the delicate balance between being sincere and yet not being devastated by being less than perfect. It is reaching forward—not living in the past or looking back, but moving forward with God.

God understands the involvements of every circumstance, and He deals accordingly. He knows what to require from every situation. He determines the level of expectation for women keeping house on dirt floors compared with those keeping house in homes with linoleum floors. He understands the handicaps and difficulties we each face as well as what we really want in our hearts. That applies to anything from earning a living to putting money in the offering. "For if there be first a willing mind, it is accepted according to that a man hath, and not according to that he hath not" (2 Corinthians 8:12).

Naturally, we need to be concerned lest we be satisfied with ourselves when God is not satisfied. We should not hide behind the "nobody's perfect" line. We must always stay open to what God wants to do in our lives. But perfection lies in the desires and intents of our hearts, not just in our accomplishments.

Perhaps this is what God meant in Hebrews 12:5, 6: "My son, despise not thou the chastening of the Lord, nor faint when thou art rebuked of him: for whom the Lord loveth he chasteneth, and scourgeth every son whom he receiveth."

In being "free indeed," we should seek for the place where we can be comfortable yet growing. We need to be satisfied that we tried sufficiently and conscientiously enough and are now content to leave the rest with the Lord. That will set us free from trying to measure ourselves through the eyes of others.

Humility is the balance for perfectionism. It helps us to understand the difference between what we are doing for the Lord and what we are doing just to impress others. Humility enables us to accept our humanity rather than needing to be extra special. It allows God to help us become what we are striving to be.

Humility allows us to be ourselves, yet be free in heart and soul, because we are trusting and walking with Him! That is being "free indeed"!

CHAPTER
TWENTY-EIGHT

Freedom by Faith

"Let not your heart be troubled: ye believe in God, believe also in me" (John 14:1).

The last chapter of a book is usually the hardest to write. To bring a sense of closure, the book should not only summarize the past and present but also project a vision of the future.

The last scene of a person's life is like that too. While reading of the final words of Moses or of the final days of Jesus before His crucifixion, it is not hard to enter into the pathos of the moment. Both scenes not only bring closure to the present era, but also point the reader into the future, showing a clear path to the Father God.

The apostle John dedicated five chapters (13–17) to the last night, the last discourse, the Last Supper, the last intimate encounters of Jesus with His own. He knew what was ahead for Him, and He knew what was ahead for them. The pleasantness of the past was gone, and a new chapter, a new era, was about to begin. He had spent the last three years developing and making disciples of His followers. Now He was leaving them.

What would He give them for direction and encouragement? He poured out His heart to them to help prepare them for the future. He pled with them to look to Him even after He would be gone.

In the earlier chapters of this book, many present difficulties of life were discussed. The closing question is, What can be said to help us to face the future with freedom? What legacy of truth can shine as a beacon to those who seek God for direction and answers?

Is there any help in these five chapters from the Book of John for finding emotional freedom? Did Jesus have these needs on His mind? Did He include directions that would aid in emotional stability in the coming days, weeks, months, and even centuries and millenniums? Would His help be sufficient for whatever lay ahead?

Interestingly, among Jesus' last words before His crucifixion, we have helps for the concluding chapter of this book. In fact, Jesus' prayer in John 17:20 includes you and me today, for He prayed, "Neither pray I for these alone, but for them also which shall believe on me through their word." I repeat, dear fellow believer, that prayer is for us! His personal prayer makes His final directions and encouragements personal to us as well.

The Need for Faith

Jesus knew what lay ahead for His disciples. He made no secret about it. "These things have I spoken unto you, that ye should not be offended. They shall put you out of the synagogues: yea, the time cometh, that whosoever killeth you will think that he doeth God service. And these things will they do unto you, because they have not known the Father, nor me. But these things have I told you, that when the time shall come, ye may remember that I told you of them. And these things I said not unto you at the beginning, because I was with you. But now I go my way to him that sent me; and none of you asketh me, Whither goest thou?" (John 16:1–5).

What was Jesus' answer to this? He had given it earlier that evening, in our caption verse, "Ye believe in God, believe also in me." *Faith* was the answer, the only answer, the enduring answer!

How powerful would this answer be? What would it do for them? Would it help them to survive just by the skin of their teeth? Or could they have "rivers of living water" flowing out of them, and could they have the abundant life, as He had said earlier, in John 7:38 and John 10:10?

Just before His last prayer with them in the upper room and before going to the Garden of Gethsemane, Jesus said, "These things I have spoken unto you, that in me ye might have peace. In the world ye shall have tribulation: but be of good cheer; I have overcome the world" (John 16:33).

Peace and good cheer! What a powerful, soothing combination—right in the midst of all that lay ahead for His disciples. His answer would meet all their needs, including their emotional ones.

Jesus had laid the groundwork earlier, when He said, "Believe in Me." He meant, "Trust Me; have faith." No doubt His disciples remembered how often He had talked to them before about believing God. Surely they drew heavily from this in the days and years that followed. Surely it steadied their convictions, their confidence, and even their emotions.

Life has not changed much. No one can have real emotional freedom without faith in God, because there are too many uncertainties and storms in life that we cannot control or avoid.

We have many legitimate spiritual concerns for ourselves, our posterity, our friends, and all others. We have concern for the faithfulness of God's people. There are physical needs we are concerned about. Those concerns and apprehensions all contain a certain amount of emotional pressure that we must deal with.

Then there are the things we do not know about the future. Jesus had warned how the future would affect many in time to come. "Men's hearts failing them for fear, and for looking after those things which are coming on the earth" (Luke 21:26). A friend put it very aptly: "The world news is not encouraging." Some people turn it off in their minds. Some can't, so they do other things to escape reality. It is not unusual for people to feel overwhelmed, especially when they don't have the Lord to turn to.

But the facts do not go away.

My realization that not all was well in the world came to me early in our local grade school. It was during the Korean War, and our school had air raid drills. The bells clanged, the lights were put out, the shades were quickly drawn, and we raced to the basement and huddled against the wall. The tensions and uncertainties in the world have not gone away since then. Many have had more difficult experiences in the real world than I ever did.

Jesus tried to instill faith in His followers for the present and future. It is always encouraging to see it lived out in real life.

An Example of Faith

The apostle Paul gave us a living example when he was on his way to Rome as a prisoner. He had warned the captain that sailing was becoming too dangerous and had advised him not to travel on. And he told the mariners, "Sirs, I perceive that this voyage will be with hurt and much damage, not only of the lading and ship, but also of our lives" (Acts 27:10).

But they went anyway. Ere long, they ran into a storm that forced them to reinforce the ship. They threw overboard everything they could to lighten the ship. They were desperate. We are told in Acts 27:20, "And when neither sun nor stars in many days appeared, and no small tempest lay on us, all hope that we should be saved was then taken away." This went on for at least fourteen days, during which the Bible says nothing about Paul. He was in the background.

Finally, he spoke, "Sirs, ye should have hearkened unto me, and not have loosed from Crete, and to have gained this harm and loss. And now I exhort you to be of good cheer: for there shall be no loss of any man's life among you, but of the ship. For there stood by me this night the angel of God, whose I am, and whom I serve, saying, Fear not, Paul; thou must be brought before Caesar: and, lo, God hath given thee all them that sail with thee. Wherefore, sirs, be of good cheer: for I believe God, that it shall be even as it was told me."

Be of good cheer when they had been pounded relentlessly by a fierce storm for over two weeks and no end was in sight? when all hope was gone?

Paul's answer was the answer of faith. Everything else had failed. He said, "I believe God." He spoke with confidence and courage. It was contagious; verse 36 tells us that all the others became of good cheer too!

That is the kind of people we want to be. We want to have the kind of buoyancy and freedom Paul had. We want to believe in God like that too.

Many others since then did not physically survive the storms of life that tested their faith. But they survived spiritually and died triumphantly in Christ. They died in loyal love for their Master. Paul himself was called to die for the Lord later.

Where does such faith come from?

The Foundation of Faith

Faith has a foundation. It is not a leap in the dark without knowing which way we are going. It is more like a child leaping into his father's arms from the upper bunk bed, or like a child in his mother's arms, oblivious to the surrounding danger.

God has always wanted man to believe in Him. He wants to be like a trusted father and mother to mankind. He wants believers to have confidence in Him. Was there ever a place as safe and secure as the Garden of Eden? Has there ever been a better place than being close to Him?

Man has always had a problem believing in that which he cannot see. God remedied that by showing mankind Himself through His Son. Jesus was not only God's messenger; He was God incarnate. When the disciples complained to Jesus that they could not perceive the Father, Jesus said, "Believe me that I am in the Father, and the Father in me: or else believe me for the very works' sake" (John 14:11). His miracles amply proved that there is a God.

Then too, creation is proof of Almighty God. God used it as a strong witness of Himself—so strong that its reality is burned into everyone's conscience and becomes a condemning point in God's judgment on man. Consider this from Romans 1:20: "For the invisible things of him from the creation of the world are clearly seen, being understood by the things that are made, even his eternal power and Godhead; so that they are without excuse."

God also reveals Himself in the Scriptures, which He confirmed by sending Jesus, the "living Word" spoken of in John 1:14. God gave us the written Word in such a way that its authority is undeniable. "Knowing this first, that no prophecy of the scripture is of any private interpretation. For the prophecy came not in old time by the will of man: but holy men of God spake as they were moved by the Holy Ghost" (2 Peter 1:20, 21).

In fact, reading the Bible is better than getting a personal revelation with our own eyes or ears. When Peter wrote of having heard God's audible voice, he added, "We have also a more sure word of prophecy" (2 Peter 1:19). This sure word is the Bible, the Word of God.

The Bible is the foundation for faith. When we accept and believe it, it does a spiritual work in us. The apostle Peter described it as seed. "Being born again, not of corruptible seed, but of incorruptible, by the word of God, which liveth and abideth for ever" (1 Peter 1:23).

How do we gain faith? Is it an act of sheer willpower? Can we *make* ourselves have such faith that gives freedom?

Getting faith results from a combination: God works in us, and we open our hearts to Him. John 1:12 gives the formula: "But as many as received him, to them gave he power to become the sons of God, even to them that believe on his name." We believe; He gives the power!

In that sense, faith is a gift. When men and women respond to Him, there is a supernatural connection to God. Jesus said again and again that faith is the link to Him. "Jesus said unto him, If thou canst believe, all things are possible to him that believeth. And straightway the father of the child cried out, and said with tears, Lord, I believe; help thou my unbelief" (Mark 9:23).

When Jesus told His disciples in the upper room, "Be of good cheer; I have overcome the world," He meant that cheer was far deeper than mere cheerfulness and good feeling. Cheer means confidence—strong courage and calm comfort. It is a deep and solid trust in God because it has a strong foundation.

Nothing pleases God like being believed in. He has told us so. "But without faith it is impossible to please him: for he that cometh to God must believe that he is, and that he is a rewarder of them that diligently seek him" (Hebrews 11:6). The gap between us and God can only be bridged by faith.

What does faith do for us in the emotional realm?

The Freedom of Faith

What kind of freedom are we hoping for? What kind of freedom did we have as children? Did we worry or even think about our next meal? Did we wonder if we would suddenly be deserted and left desolate by our parents? Probably not. There was unparalleled freedom in childhood. Maybe that is why Jesus kept using innocent, trusting children as an example of what adult believers are to be like.

Perhaps the most significant hallmark of childlike faith is the acceptance of its own vulnerability. For example, children have faith in their parents without even comprehending risk or danger. Perfect peace is theirs while tucked in the crook of the arm, even though the risk of falling exists all the while. Remember how Mephibosheth was not saved from injury while in the arms of his nurse.

Because of children's acceptance of vulnerability and their simple, uncluttered faith, Christ pointed to them as examples for our faith. Although these freedoms of childhood pass, the need for childlike faith in God never does.

We cannot truly have faith in God without accepting our own vulnerability and the possibility of difficulty that comes along with it. If life had no problems too big for us, we would not need faith. Neither can we truly trust God without a sense of awe that has confidence in His unexplainable ways. As a child trusts his adult guardian, we need to trust in the living God.

Although childhood freedom passes, God's promises and presence with His own never do. He is able to be much more to His own than any adult can be to any child. Faith in the power of His promises produces a freedom that never passes away. How we need that!

Faith does not necessarily come easily. One man said it takes great trials to make strong faith. Facing those trials requires a close walk with the Lord, trusting everything to Him.

Here are some of the blessings of freedom by faith:

Freedom by faith trusts everything to God. Faith finds its rest by surrendering all things to Him "who worketh all things after the counsel of his own will" (Ephesians 1:11).

Freedom by faith lets God have His way even when we don't understand.

Freedom by faith enables us to live. Faith considers every day to be a manifestation of His goodness to us.

Freedom by faith counts it a privilege to serve the Lord—to be a part of His eternal purposes on the earth and in the world to come!

Freedom by faith anticipates the return of the Lord Jesus, who said, "I will come again, and receive you unto myself; that where I am, there ye may be also" (John 14:3).

Freedom by faith gives confidence for the present. When we are assured that He is with us and we are with Him, we are able to look to the future with confidence as well.

The poet James Wells put it so well:

Living by Faith

I care not today what tomorrow may bring,
If shadow or sunshine or rain;
The Lord I know ruleth o'er everything,
And all of my worry is vain.

Though tempests may blow and the storm clouds arise,
Obscuring the brightness of life;
I'm never alarmed at the overcast skies,
The Master looks on at the strife.

I know that He safely will carry me through,
No matter what evils betide;
Why should I then care though the tempest may blow,
If Jesus walks close to my side.

Our Lord will return to this earth some sweet day,
Our troubles will then all be o'er;
The Master so gently will lead us away,
Beyond that blest heavenly shore.

Chorus:
Living by faith, in Jesus above,
Trusting, confiding in His great love;
From all harm safe in His sheltering arm,
I'm living by faith, and feel no alarm.